# Virtue-Based
# Restorative Discipline

# Virtue-Based Restorative Discipline

## A Catholic Response to Bullying Behavior

By Lynne Lang

# Table of Contents

# Preface

*He said to them, "It is not for you to know times or seasons*
*which the Father has fixed by his own authority.*
*But you shall receive power when the Holy Spirit*
*has come upon you; and you shall be my witnesses*
*in Jerusalem and in all Judea and Sama'ria*
*and to the end of the earth."*

Acts 1:7-8

MY MOTHER LOVES TO TELL THE STORY of my persistence in convincing
her to allow me to join the "School Safety Patrol" when selected by my
teacher at age ten.

"Absolutely not — that is too dangerous! You could get hurt or killed
by a car. What if someone has brake failure while you are in the street?"
Her small Italian frame bounced with animation, and her words rattled
with emotion as she painted this vivid image of my demise. Yet my firm
resolution to help direct my fellow students across the street to safety
seemed a mission of greater purpose, and I was eventually able to persuade her to have a change of heart.

The student patrols were required to sign a safety pledge, agreeing
to provide safety and to act responsibly on behalf of others. I took great
pride in my daily duties, assuring there was a safe passage for students
crossing the street to and from Temple Terrace Elementary in 1963.
With training and supervision by wise and all-knowing teachers, my
own safety was guaranteed, and my mother's worries soon dissipated.

Now, as I reflect on those tender years and how convinced I was of
my greater purpose, I am once again feeling summoned to be in the role
of directing you, my readers, through the passages you may face in handling conflict and repairing harm in relationships. I am simply a traffic
director, watching to make sure the way is clear for your journey and
preparing you to approach and cross those intersections where conflict
meets solution with thought and care, guided by the Holy Spirit. I don't

know what the journey holds, but I can guarantee the lessons and information herein will provide a sure guide along your journey to the other side. Despite the dangerous "traffic" and the conditions you may face, expect the good companionship of Jesus along the way, equipping you with the power of love and forgiveness. As surely as the sun rises, there will be difficulties in even the best of relationships. And as surely as the sun sets, you can count on a personal, profound God to be a constant source of wisdom and hope for all who seek him.

This guide will provide you with the solid foundation to understand the inextricable link between faith and discipline. However, the principles and practices of Virtue-Based Restorative Discipline™ (VBRD™) are meant to be a way of life. They express a deeper link between each of us and the covenant love of a merciful Master. For those readers wishing for their schools to become VBRD™ certified, there are training services, ongoing networking, technical support, and surveys to measure effectiveness.

Go to the VBRD™ Web site for information about training dates and other resources: www.virtuebase.org

# Foreword

*"I keep thinking of Queen Esther who was taken away from her people precisely because God wanted her to plead with the king on behalf of her nation. I am a very poor and powerless little Esther, but the King who has chosen me is infinitely great and merciful."*

Saint Teresa Benedicta of the Cross

---

AUGUST 9, 2012

IT WAS THE BUSIEST TIME OF THE YEAR FOR SCHOOLS. Opening buildings and preparing for the first day of school is a time of wonder and hope. The date was set for our first formal training in Saint Louis; it was the only date the room was available for a group as large as 150. That represented twenty-seven schools from the Archdiocese of Saint Louis, bringing teams to learn the steps in this first year of a formal pilot for VBRD™.

One of my practices over the years in working with Catholic schools has been to study the saint whose feast day happens to land on the date of my trainings. Today was no exception, but it seemed uncanny that this particular training date fell on such a significant feast day, because this work of school peace and safety seems to be God's special project assigned to my care:

AUGUST 9 — *Feast day of Edith Stein, Saint Teresa Benedicta of the Cross*
In my preparation for that day's work, I spent extra time learning about this woman. I was humbled to learn of her acceptance of death as a Jew, even though she was a professed Catholic Carmelite. The significance of this was noted on the day of her beatification in Vatican documents regarding her sainthood:

"When Edith Stein was beatified in Cologne on 1 May 1987, the Church honored 'a daughter of Israel,' as Pope John Paul II put it, who, as a Catholic during Nazi persecution, remained faithful to the crucified Lord Jesus Christ and, as a Jew, to her people in loving faithfulness."

Edith Stein's gracious acceptance in all circumstances has been inspiring. She truly was filled with joy as she spent her life for the cause of peace:

"Even now I accept the death that God has prepared for me in complete submission and with joy as being his most holy will for me. I ask the Lord to accept my life and my death ... so that the Lord will be accepted by his people and that his kingdom may come in glory, for the salvation of Germany and the peace of the world," she said in her will.[1]

So the cause of joyfully bringing God's peace is one that has fallen into my hands in this work. Further, the miracles that brought about her beatification are equally significant. They are those wrought out of the suffering within families who prayed for miracles in her name. The Reverend Charles McCarthy, founder of the Center for Christian Nonviolence, tells the most compelling story about the miracle that saved his young daughter's life at precisely the time he was celebrating the closing remarks of his first retreat for nonviolence in Minnesota. He and hundreds of others had been prayerfully interceding for of his dying daughter, commending her to the loving care of Edith Stein, and the future saint did not disappoint this desperate father, his family, and their prayer companions. His faith had saved his small daughter, a miracle declared by her attending physician — the final action to move Edith to sainthood. I encourage readers to discover more

---

1. Teresa Benedict of the Cross Edith Stein (1891-1942), Discalced Carmelite, martyr. www.vatican.va/news_services/liturgy/saints/ns_lit_doc_19981011_edith_stein_en.html

about the life of Saint Teresa Benedicta of the Cross through the many good resources available.

A special thank you is in order to those schools that beautifully practiced virtues of patience, hope, and faith throughout the time of discernment and formation that has shaped this work. Thank you to every person who been an audience to my presentations, learned what I attempted to teach about this work, and put it into practice. I may never meet you, but I am grateful for the collective spirit and energy around VBRD™.

Margaret Ahle, it all began with our conversation about your amazing school, Holy Trinity. Your pastor, the Reverend Paul Niemann, and your dedicated staff followed your lead. Nina Ashby and Sandy Selvaggi, thank you for standing at the forefront of this work with the students. Marianne Jones, the dedicated principal at Good Shepherd School, and her good pastor, the Reverend Chris Holtmann, have led a most amazing journey that has borne much fruit. John Frietag, your support as principal of Saint Peter School, Kirkwood, Missouri, along with that of my beloved pastor, Msgr. Jack Costello, have been invaluable. This could not have been as thorough in its content without Anne Loida, the teacher whose organization and implementation of staff circles confirmed the benefits of that process.

Principal Susie Rohrer from Saint Joseph School knew there was something missing in her school "spirit," and says the school has never been the same, thanks to her willingness to talk about changing hearts among her staff and students. Her teachers inspired me to continue the work as I watched them making big changes. A special thanks to Jamie AuBuchon for her energy and enthusiasm and to Stephanie Rayoum for serving on the team.

Saint Simon School, under the leadership of Sharon Lenger, has helped to shape the training into best practices by bringing the entire staff to a VBRD™ class. We are learning together about what works and what needs work for successful implementation. Thank you.

Of course, teachers such as Doris Skoff, Sarah Reed, and Rob Westling have led teams, faculties, and students to new depths in implementation to further the cause of this important work. And how could

I fail to mention the good people at Saint Peter in Kirkwood who have taught me everything I need to know about love! Thank you Nancy Brown, Christy Patritti, Kathleen Carmody, and a special thanks to Kristen Figge for her willingness to walk the extra mile(s) with me. You all have taught me about parent circles and trusted me with your uncertainty. The virtue of faith has been evident in this work.

Archbishop Robert J. Carlson has been a wonderful shepherd for Saint Louis, and history will surely celebrate his bold leadership in initiating the mission advancement campaign for Catholic education, *Alive in Christ!* The New Evangelization has provided a rich opportunity to see the movement of the Holy Spirit in many ways, and this compass keeps us mindful of our deeper call. My good colleagues in our Catholic Education Center have been helpful in more ways than I can begin to express. Thanks go to Mr. George Henry, for your dedication and leadership as superintendent of our Catholic schools; Msgr. John Unger, for listening and helping give shape to this vision; Mr. Al Winkelmann, my boss, and a great model of loyalty and dedication! Dr. Karen Tichy, thanks for your tough questions and great intellect. Mrs. Denny Bram, you made me do it! I've prayed for discernment and guidance for more than ten years as we moved the hearts of some of our teachers to be more loving and kind. Thank you for pushing me to go to the hard place. Julie Phelps, what a tenderhearted, dedicated, beautiful person you are to help me organize trainings and materials, manuals, etc. Thank you to all the office staff — you pull together to help one another. Dr. Ed Hogan of the Pontifical Institute has been a good spiritual guide and companion, and I am grateful for his support and effort in ensuring the accuracy of my work.

A very special thanks to my team: Dr. John James from Saint Louis University; Dr. Tracy James, his wife; Tim and Kristen Figge; and my amazingly helpful daughter, Rachel, for the countless hours of help with filming and editing videos, and with book design and Web site work. To Nick, Ali, Audrey, and Joe, you've been my best teachers about love and forgiveness. Thank you.

Finally, thanks to Gary, my beloved husband, for modeling the virtues of patience, kindness, temperance, forbearance, and docility.

# CHAPTER 1

## INTRODUCTION

*"Jesus then said to the Jews who had believed in him,*
*'If you continue in my word, you are truly my disciples, and you*
*will know the truth, and the truth will make you free.'"*

John 8:31-32

WELCOME TO A SPIRITUAL APPROACH to disciplining that cultivates virtue and provides a rich foundation for fostering faith both at home and at school. If a child struggles with behavior at school, many times that struggle starts at home. Parents are seeking answers. They must rely on a partnership with school personnel to bring a seamless, consistent message of the profound goodness of the human person. This very notion may cause us to feel a bit guilty as we think of our impatient tirades and outbursts, which are certainly not our proudest parenting moments. Have you ever considered that every thought, every word and every deed is a step toward, or away from, heaven? Some of us rarely consider the divine as we navigate our daily lives.

Believing in the profound goodness of each human person, the desire for true happiness, and longing for heaven may sound like ideals as you consider some of the challenging people and circumstances you encounter. After all, you are surrounded on every side by complaints, criticism, and judgment. In the natural world, we are faced with practical problems daily: running late for school or work, mechanical failures, routine maintenance. Then, there are interpersonal conflicts that may lead to irreconcilable differences. At times, these can be the biggest barriers to enabling the supernatural to become evident. How many times do we rush to get our day going, making sure everyone is awake, fed, dressed, and ready, and yet fail to see the supernatural in these mundane tasks? Every circumstance is placed before us as an opportunity to evangelize; unfortunately, these opportunities don't always come in attractive, user-friendly packaging!

According to Dictionary.com, virtue is moral excellence; righteousness; goodness. *The Catechism of the Catholic Church* (*CCC*) defines virtue as:

> A virtue is an habitual and firm disposition to do the good. It allows the person not only to perform good acts, but to give the best of himself. The virtuous person tends toward the good with all his sensory and spiritual powers; he pursues the good and chooses it in concrete actions.
>
> The goal of a virtuous life is to become like God. (1803)

*def of virtue*

The simplest definition I share with children and adults is this: Virtue is a holy habit that imitates God. If you think of people you know who possess such habits, chances are they have deep faith. This sourcebook can inspire you to cultivate a truer sense of God's holy presence within yourself and within those you influence. For example, if you were to take a moment and find someone close by, offering a smile and a kind word, that simple act would most likely yield a smile and kindness in return. A small act that is directed to the good is virtuous. Those less-than-proud parenting moments you have are not virtuous. When we apologize for such behavior, however, we are practicing humility and temperance, to name just two virtues. When I think of such instances, I am reminded of the numerous times a dear priest friend, the Reverend

Sam Martin, said, "God can bring about good in any situation!" Scripture supports this idea. Even our parenting failures can bring about good, especially when we are encouraged to consider practicing acts that help us intentionally imitate God:

> We know that in everything God works for good with those who love him, who are called according to his purpose. (*Romans* 8:28)

Virtues are holy habits that imitate God and set you on a path to intimacy with the Creator. They also may inspire good in return, but we must continue seeking the supernatural, lest we catch ourselves feeling we deserve to be treated with reciprocity. Just because you choose to act kindly doesn't necessarily mean you will always receive kindness in return. Look at the kindness of Jesus. Was his kindness reciprocated? No — he was crucified. But he was so aligned with his Father that he operated at a higher frequency, recognizing both the human and the divine forces at work. Just as our relationships on earth are dynamic and changing over time, our relationship to God is also dynamic. The difference is that God is the ever-present, all-knowing, unchanging force of divine love. The change happens within us as we discover more about that divine love.

The ethics of virtue predate Christianity. Early philosophers were prophetic in their message about "living for good." Socrates outlined a foundation for living 400 years before the birth of Christ. Many of the beliefs we embrace today came from this foundation. My faith journey as a Catholic has led me to understand that these virtues can inspire us in our heavenly journey. In simple yet profound ways, I was influenced by some of the spiritual giants in my life as I listened to and watched them, allowing God to reveal his truth about them and through them.

You may have heard the word "virtue" without thinking too much about what it actually means. I was first awakened to the language of virtue long after my childhood. Virtues surround us from our earliest memories as we reflect on the Ten Commandments, our spiritual gifts through the sacraments, Scripture, and simple everyday conversations. If virtue is so prevalent in our everyday world, how could I have missed it? Simply put, it was not lived in an intentional way.

The Holy Spirit worked through Cardinal Raymond Burke, whom I met first as the bishop of the Diocese of LaCrosse, Wisconsin, in 2002. Somehow, his clear distinction of what God was doing in the lives of people around him helped me to see the personal holiness that results from living a holy life. For instance, he openly identified and named virtues observed in those around him. In turn, this enabled me to recognize the holiness in others. Perhaps readers understand this idea already, but I was missing part of the formula in striving for heaven.

Personal holiness is evident not just in seeking God, but seeking God in others, too (loving God, loving neighbor). It sounds simple enough, but Cardinal Burke's message opened a new corridor of faith for me. It is the spoken word that makes all the difference. We might say, "thanks for that," or "that was really nice." But would we think to say, "Thank you! Your generosity was extraordinary — that virtue is a blessing," or "What a work of mercy! Thank you!" It is the difference between seeing the good and experiencing the impact of the goodness.

As Cardinal Burke spoke of the everyday world around him in this way, his words directed me to a supernatural world that drew me to a greater sense of mission for my daily life. The Holy Spirit was nudging me to a closer walk with Christ, urging me to step into deeper waters in my faith journey. Not only was I responsible for living a "good" life, I was being called to a better life — one that would entirely change my journey to eternity. Those everyday experiences provided a challenge to deepen my reflection on God's will for my life, and to see my work as a personal invitation by God — my call to evangelization.

A call to evangelization is a call to intimacy with Christ, and a call to bring the salvation message of Christ to others. We are wired to share God's perfect love, all-forgiving and all-giving, every day in every circumstance, big and small.

The witness of a Christian life and good works done in a supernatural spirit have great power to draw men to the faith and to God. (*CCC* 2044)

As I began this interior, reflective journey, it changed my outward approach to working with people in the field of violence prevention. My work in this field had begun ten years earlier when my children were teens. I was confident there was so much we could do to bring hope for the future, and God directed my path to writing health curricula for students. However, it didn't take long to see that our schools are a microcosm of society, and that the problems with school violence clearly begin with adults — because children learn their conflict skills at the earliest ages from watching their parents.

As a result, I began to place more emphasis on training adults and eventually developed this Virtue-Based Restorative Discipline (VBRD™) model for addressing bullying and other disruptive behaviors. By surveying students, parents, and school personnel, we were able to provide evidence that this approach was changing hearts and minds (and behaviors) in Catholic school communities, and it was being well-received.

In my work with a large, secular hospital network as a writer and trainer in school health, I helped to build and shape a staff of more than a dozen educators over a fourteen-year period under the leadership of Mrs. Diana Wilhold, a champion for healthy children. While we developed health curricula for all areas of youth health, my specialization became violence prevention, which grew into the urgent issue of school bullying. Our team of educators reached more than seventy thousand young people annually with the message that this behavior was unacceptable. We pioneered ideas and beliefs that celebrated the goodness of all children at a time when schools were pushing for zero-tolerance policies, and states were mandated to enact legislation that attempted to empty schools of "bullies." These unforgiven souls were left to find alternative learning environments. It seemed as though we were disposing of these young people, thinking they would disappear from the face of the earth. However, they showed up later to bag our groceries or work in corporations, and they resurfaced in neighborhoods and churches and at community events. They didn't go away, and we held on to the memories of the circumstances under which they left. Tragically, we offered them no way to return to goodness, and we never strengthened those targeted by their cruelty to build confidence and skill in articulating their distress and learning resiliency.

Over time, I became more troubled by this idea of banishing children. When I shared the message that bullying was not kind, nor was unkindness any part of God's plan, I realized that the newfound zeal I had was affecting people in profound ways. For me, the interior change inspired by Cardinal Burke became a hunger for daily Mass, more personal prayer and reflection, and a desire to tell others what God was doing in my life. I found myself incorporating prayer and Scripture, and reading from papal letters and encyclicals — and all that became part of my presentations in schools. I was finding the link between these documents and peacekeeping in schools.

Even though I was working for a secular employer, Catholic schools kept calling me to assist them in their efforts to address bullying. Public schools and private schools had unique needs respective to safety and violence prevention, and I was drawn to begin addressing my audiences with a message that was primarily directed to end the decline in Catholic school enrollment. Over and over again, families expressed feelings of being marginalized, ignored, and shunned. There was little physical bullying, but the exclusion was unbearable. More than once I heard, "Public schools show more Christian behavior than Catholic schools." These families did not feel the love of God from their neighbors in school and parish communities. Upon reporting the painful experiences their children faced, they felt little or no support or improvement in their circumstance.

In public schools, if a child is marginalized, there are other places to go for acceptance: community-based extracurricular activities and church and neighborhood community events. In Catholic communities, however, if a child is marginalized or bullied at school, that same experience can spill over into the sports teams and scout groups and even affect church attendance. Even the fish fries during Lent can be a source of pain  A parent once stated, "If my child doesn't fit in at school, she won't fit in anywhere here at this parish." Is it possible that these families not only leave our schools, but leave our churches — and their Catholic faith practices, too? I believe God can use any circumstance as a call to evangelization for both those harmed and those responsible for the harm. Both ends of the bullying spectrum need our help and support.

As this work began in schools, it did not take long for those I have worked with to see the change to which God is calling us:

- Some of those people struggling to fit in found peace as they prayed and began practicing virtue; people shared that as they met the challenge to cultivate virtue, beginning with themselves, they were changing for the better.

- Some expressed a need to revisit old relationships and conversations to seek or grant forgiveness.

- Some shared teary-eyed tales of ways God was touching them during our prayer and reflection; one woman confided that she needed to return to the sacraments and was feeling remorse for the way she had failed to forgive God for her life circumstances.

- One teacher expressed that the time together was positively changing even the hardest hearts among the staff.

- One non-Catholic chose to convert after experiencing the love and the faith shared among her peers in the school.

Just imagine the possibilities when members of school communities become better at creating a culture of kindness within their homes, their classrooms, in faculty lounges, and in the parking lot in everyday conversations with and about others. Gossip could be eliminated. These changes are the fruit of virtue. Virtue inspires goodness — that's how we know we are on the right track.

Each reader of this work is capable of bearing this same fruit. There are many ways God reaches us, and this is simply one avenue. God tirelessly seeks us through all of creation in new ways as we encounter divinity through the human experience:

> The steadfast love of the LORD never ceases,
> his mercies never come to an end;
> they are new every morning;
> great is thy faithfulness. (*Lamentations* 3:22-23)

I realized I had been failing to tell people that my work was my call to evangelization. Initially, I stated this notion about my work almost apologetically. After all, Catholics are not always comfortable talking intimately about their faith. One other point about Cardinal Burke's wisdom is this: He stated that we must always be willing to invite others to a deeper faith. In speaking of vocations, he noted, "We must ask young people, 'Have you thought about the priesthood or the consecrated life?'"

When the demand for my work continued to grow, it was evidence that school communities were seeking answers to end bullying. It didn't take long for me to add to the message about my call to evangelization: "It's your call to evangelization, too." I felt compelled to encourage others to consider sharing the call to journey with Christ. As the *Catechism* teaching on evangelization states, our supernatural experiences have the power to draw others to faith and to God:

Lay people fulfill their prophetic mission by evangelization:

> This witness of life, however, is not the sole element in the apostolate; the true apostle is on the lookout for occasions of announcing Christ by word, either to unbelievers . . . or to the faithful. (*CCC* 905)

So now we can challenge one another to work shoulder to shoulder in the vineyard as companions for the journey! Over time, I began to state this in my presentations: "I know this is my call to evangelization, and I believe that some of you listening may discover that it is yours, too. If we are to keep our Catholic schools open, fill our churches and enjoy a future for Catholics here, it is up to each of us to discover that call within ourselves."

As parents and staff continued to work with me to prevent bullying, we all realized we were becoming better people and were encouraged by the changes in school culture that we were witnessing. Yet there was a missing ingredient in the recipe for kindness in Catholic school culture. Kindness is the fruit of living out our Catholic identity. If we talk about the message and fail to talk about the messenger, we've missed the mark. As I learned from *The Hidden Power of Kindness*, by Lawrence Lovasik,[2] there is no such thing as a "random act of kindness." Every act is intentional, because all kindness comes from God, the creator of divine kindness. So, our God's ultimate act of kindness was sending his son, Jesus, to live and die for us. How kind is that? Someone has paid the price for our mistakes — even before we make them. Every act of kindness we commit is a response to God's love and kindness toward us, because he first loved us. This is good news. Evangelization is sharing the good news! But many times we miss it entirely. Right?

*Kindness never "random act"*

Just take a look around you. In our Catholic schools, we may be attempting to duplicate the local public education with a little added prayer. We may gloss over the precepts of faith and teach religion as though it was a subject separate from the whole of our lives. It is time to reveal God's glory so powerfully that it spills into hallways, lunchrooms, playgrounds, and anywhere else two or more are gathered.

> It is too little a thing that you should be my servant to raise up the tribes of Jacob and to restore the preserved of Israel; I will give you as a light to the nations, that my salvation may reach to the end of the earth. (*Isaiah* 49:6)

By bringing virtue into focus, we are evangelizing because we are thinking, speaking, and acting in response to the goodness of God in everyday life. This is our response to the gifts we have been given,

---

2. Lawrence G. Lovasik, *The Hidden Power of Kindness: A Practical Handbook for Souls Who Dare to Transform the World, One Deed at a Time* (Manchester, NH: Sophia Institute Press, 1999).

because all good things come from God, and virtue is living out that goodness.

Relationships must be seen as invitations to grow in grace — for everyone involved. We must also be mindful of those good and kind students who innocently witness, and are victimized by, the poor behavior that happens on playgrounds everywhere, every day. High accountability and responsibility for making relationships the most important aspect of school life can foster the conversations critical to bringing peace within hearts and hallways everywhere. With academic standards and achievement as a high priority, a positive school climate demands new, innovative ways to address interpersonal conflict. VBRD™ can provide a comprehensive, systemic approach to improving school climate, thereby fostering an environment of safety and academic success. This initiative will address those intentional, mean-spirited acts of harm, those targeted by these acts, and those who witness them. Adults at home and at school can create a consistent message of hope by actively cultivating virtue and holding relationships as the highest priority.

# CHAPTER 2

## THE CRITICAL ROLE OF SCHOOL CLIMATE

*"Thy steadfast love, O LORD, endures for ever."*

Psalm 138:8

SCHOOL CLIMATE IS THE OVERALL EXPERIENCE within any given day at school. It begins with the voice on the phone and the face of the door attendant, and it ends with the last impression one has when leaving a building. Jane Bluestein, Ph.D., author of *Creating Emotionally Safe Schools*,[3] has developed an exhaustive checklist for reflection on human interactions between adults and children. Bluestein's list includes such qualities as autonomy, respect and dignity, limits, positive consequences, and emotional safety. Expecting educators to create and maintain this type of environment and providing them with the appropriate training takes dedicated effort. Within each category listed in her book are clear identifiers for fulfilling the emotional needs of students; in turn, that can foster academic success. Though lacking faith components, and Catholic iden-

---

3. Jane Bluestein, *Creating Emotionally Safe Schools: A Guide for Educators and Parents* (Deerfield, FL: HCI Books, 2001).

tity in particular, Bluestein's concepts nevertheless challenge schools to thoughtfully consider daily practices.

Emotional safety can be described as a sense of belonging and acceptance and having the freedom and support to both succeed and to fail. The many dimensions of school climate are the delicate balance (similar to a recipe) of conditions on any given day that form an overall positive or negative experience. How others support or insulate one another in the negative experiences further contributes to or detracts from one's sense of emotional safety. A positive school climate holds emotional needs and the quality of the human experience in high regard. With this understanding, it is broader than simply "bullying prevention," and plays a more significant role because it can be the foundation of quality relationships within schools.

Bullying has had more than its fair share of attention in recent years. For our common understanding, the definition used in this book will come from two sources. Dr. Dan Olweus, creator of the Olweus Bullying Prevention Program (OBPP), provides us with this commonly accepted definition for bullying in his book, *Bullying at School: What We Know and What We Can Do*[4]:

> A person is bullied when he or she is exposed, repeatedly and over time, to negative actions on the part of one or more other persons, and he or she has difficulty defending himself or herself.

This definition includes three important components:

1. Bullying is aggressive behavior that involves unwanted, negative actions.

2. Bullying involves a pattern of behavior repeated over time.

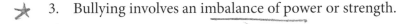 3. Bullying involves an imbalance of power or strength.

---

4. Dan Olweus, *Bullying at School: What We Know and What We Can Do (Understanding Children's Worlds)* (Hoboken, NJ: Wiley-Blackwell, 1993).

In my co-authored workbook with SuEllen Fried, *30 Activities for Getting Better at Getting Along*,[5] the definition rests on specific identifying characteristics:

1. There is intent to harm.

2. There is intensity and duration.

3. There is an imbalance of power.

4. The target is vulnerable.

5. The target is isolated and unsupported.

6. The target experiences significant consequences.

The terms typically used to label specific roles in bullying are bullies, victims, and bystanders. SuEllen and I refer to these roles, however, as bulliers, targets, and witnesses. This eliminates the "stickiness" of the bully label, the sense of vulnerability and powerlessness of being victimized, and the lack of accountability for simply "standing by."

To take this idea one step further in recognizing the overall impact of hurtful behavior, we can eliminate the use of the word "bullying" by simply using three identifying behaviors we defined when I worked with staff in the hospital-based school outreach program in Saint Louis: harm, humiliation, and intimidation.

If we were to simply talk about ways we harm, humiliate, or intimidate one another, we could be clear about what is actually happening to cause pain. Harm can be physical or emotional. Humiliation is anything that is intended to diminish human dignity, such as name-calling or negative humor (humor aimed at hurting someone, usually with a twist of sarcasm). And, finally, intimidation is a threat, whether it is withholding friendship or coercing another to surrender something such as money or possessions, or threatening to harm the target physically.

---

5. SuEllen Fried and Lynne Lang, *30 Activities for Getting Better At Getting Along* (Bully Safe USA, 2005).

Rather than labeling a person a bully, it is much easier to work at restoring relationships. By breaking down our title into "Virtue-Based" and "Restorative Discipline," we can see two converging ideas forming a new model for discipline that has two main outcomes aimed at creating and maintaining a positive school climate:

1. Decrease antisocial behaviors.

2. Increase faith practices.

Many existing programs are designed to address misbehaviors and generally are punitive. School policy may sound something like this: If you fight, you will get three demerits, or an in-school suspension. If you disrupt the classroom, you will get a checkmark, and three checks gives you an after-school detention. If you talk back to the teacher, you will stay in from recess; and so on.

The cycle repeats itself because there is no introduction of the virtue of God's justice. Many times, students report they are not in agreement with an assigned punishment, and at other times students have said that they don't even know why they are given a punishment. An adult may even attempt to defend an assigned punishment with a statement such as: "If you can't figure out why you're missing recess, then this is a good time for you to think about it!" This will be explained further in chapter 6.

Figure 1 illustrates this idea visually:

FIGURE 1

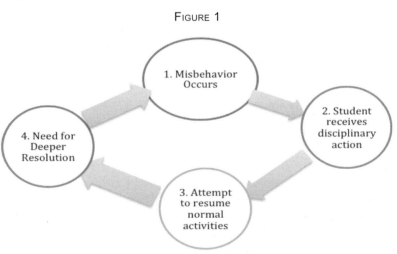

*(handwritten margin note: Goal of this program, (for bullies))*

PARENTS    STUDENTS
STAFF

FIGURE 2
Schools' success in creating the most positive climate possible depends on the stability of commitment from staff, students, and parents. Just as with a three-legged stool, when one leg is weak, it creates instability.

In the VBRD™ model, we want schools to see misbehavior in the context of the whole child, both at home and at school. Our society has become so intent on "getting the job done" that we fail to integrate our body and soul into everyday tasks. This new comprehensive model is designed to inspire everyone within a school community to grow spiritually by learning first about virtue. Then, when harm occurs, we will look at the harm caused by misbehavior and make amends within the context of faith identity. We will repair and restore relationships first because we want to live a virtuous life. We also know that becoming virtuous means loving God and neighbor, and that we want to do unto others as we would have them do unto us.

All successful efforts undertaken in any school must rely on the strong partnership of what can be described as a three-legged stool (see figure 2). In order for God's work to be done with the greatest positive outcome, all three legs must bear the weight equally. When one leg wobbles, the entire structure is compromised. These legs are parents, students, and school staff.

By analyzing the title of this book, *Virtue-Based Restorative Discipline*™ (VBRD™), we can see the value each aspect can bring to increasing faith practices and restoring relationships caused by harm. The next chapters will look at these two concepts more closely.

So how can we begin to do this? Start with Scripture, reflection and reading about virtue, and your discussions with others will hopefully inspire new ways of seeing with the eyes of your hearts. Change is possible, and when we become willing partners with God, anything is possible. When we slow the pace of our lives to reflect on our actions, it becomes clear that there is a holy longing, as the *Catechism* states:

> Deep within his conscience man discovers a law which he has not laid upon himself but which he must obey. Its voice, ever calling him to love and to do what is good and to avoid evil, sounds in his heart at the right moment. . . . For man has in his heart a law inscribed by God. . . . His conscience is man's most secret core and his sanctuary. There he is alone with God whose voice echoes in his depths. (1776)

Now let's consider looking at school climate from the perspective of lessons learned in the aftermath of school violence. In June 1999, following the attack at Columbine High School in Colorado, the U.S. Secret Service and the U.S. Department of Education began a Safe School Initiative,[6] studying 37 incidents of targeted school shootings and school attacks in the United States from 1974 through June 2000. Every aspect of the thinking, planning, and related behaviors of the student attackers was explored. The primary goal was to learn how to prevent future attacks. The results included ten key findings:

1. Incidents of targeted violence at school rarely were sudden, impulsive acts.

2. Prior to most incidents, other people knew about the attacker's idea and/or plan to attack.

3. Most attackers did not threaten their targets directly prior to advancing the attack.

---

6.   Bryan Vossekuil, Robert A. Fein, Ph.D., Marisa Reddy, Ph.D., Randy Borum, Psy.D., and William Modzeleski, *The Final Report and Findings of the Safe School Initiative: Implications for the Prevention of School Attacks in the United States* (Washington, D.C.: United States Secret Service and United States Department of Education, May 2002).

4. There is no accurate or useful "profile" of students who engaged in targeted school violence.[7]

5. Most attackers engaged in some behavior prior to the incident that caused others concern or indicated a need for help.

6. Most attackers had difficulty coping with significant losses or personal failures. Moreover, many had considered or attempted suicide.

7. Many attackers felt bullied, persecuted, or injured by others prior to the attack.

8. Most attackers had access to and had used weapons prior to the attack.

9. In many cases, other students were involved in some capacity.

10. Despite prompt law-enforcement responses, most shooting incidents were stopped by means other than law enforcement intervention.

This terrifying violence clearly may not always be predictable; yet in hindsight, these findings indicate that in many cases it is preventable. Catholic schools have unique school climate issues when compared with their public counterparts. There is significantly less physical violence, and when families cannot maintain the standards of behavior and academic performance in our private schools, they often simply leave and enroll their children in public schools.

The goal of VBRD™ is to help schools take action to restore relationships when harm occurs anywhere on the spectrum — from verbal and nonverbal incidents to more serious physical bullying.

---

7. Here the term "profile" refers to a set of demographic and other traits that a set of perpetrators of a crime have in common. Refer to "Characterizing the Attacker" in chapter 3 of *Threat Assessment in Schools Guide*, Reddy, et al. (2001), "Evaluating risk for targeted violence in schools" in the resources section for further explanation of the term "profile."

The social responsibility to respond with compassion will serve two purposes:

1.  We are doing as Jesus instructed.

2.  We are making our Catholic schools places of possibility. Among the ten key findings listed on the previous page, numbers 6 and 7 cited in the Safe School Initiative report can be helpful in recognizing the value of a positive school climate. They note that the attackers struggled to cope with loss, to the point of suicide ideation, and stated that they were targets of bullying behaviors:

*Finding 6:* Most attackers had difficulty coping with significant losses or personal failures. Moreover, many had considered or attempted suicide.

Resiliency is the ability to manage the circumstances that life presents with ease and confidence. Resiliency is a key ingredient in both violence and substance abuse prevention, thus linking undesirable behaviors with risk for other self-destructive behaviors in adolescents.[8] My background in health education began in 1994, learning about risk and protective factors, the research of Dr. Peter Benson on 40 Developmental Assets,[9] and other relevant work in the field of prevention. *Risk and Protective Factors*[10] with regard to aggressive or violent behavior are those indicators such as history of domestic violence or commitment to self-control (virtue of temperance) that can influence one's likelihood of engaging in violent acts.

The fact that most attackers lack resiliency as indicated in *Finding 6* points to a need for a shift in our educational practices to provide

---

8. "Drug Abuse Prevention," The National Institute on Drug Abuse, http://www. drugabuse.gov/publications/topics-in-brief/drug-abuse-prevention.

9. "40 Developmental Assets®," Search Institute, http://www.search-institute.org/ developmental-assets

10. "Youth Violence: Risk and Protective Factors," Centers for Disease Control and Prevention, http://www.cdc.gov/violenceprevention/youthviolence/riskprotec-tivefactors.html

critical and creative thinking skills as an integral part of learning. Who owns the learning? Do teachers, or do students? By asking questions and giving students the chance to think and problem solve, we are allowing them to own the learning. Learning facts through memorization and not applying them in practical ways contributes to the inability to creatively problem solve in healthy ways.

As one teacher pointed out during a VBRD™ training, this model meets the criteria within *Standards for English Language Arts and Literacy History/Social Studies, Science and Technical Studies for Integration of Knowledge and Ideas for Common Core Curriculum Standards*[11], and her school actually included some of the skills taught in VBRD™ in their curriculum as such. She and many others implementing VBRD™ believe that the small and large incidents that require disciplinary action in schools are effective ways to reduce harmful behavior and build resiliency because students have a way to return to goodness through VBRD™ when they cause harm. Those around them who are affected can learn to effectively articulate their distress and their need to be assured that equity will be restored and guaranteed in the future.

We must connect with the core belief that we are "very good," as the *Book of Genesis* states (see 1:31). This happens through the process of self-discovery about harm and its implications on the surrounding community. Implementing VBRD™ in its fullest capacity brings resiliency to the forefront, thus helping to identify needs among students for life-skills coaching in healthy ways to articulate distress.

In this same way, VBRD™ can contribute the measurable outcomes within the *2012 National Standards and Benchmarks for Effective Elementary and Secondary Catholic Schools, Catholic School Standard 9*, which states:

---

11. National Governors Association Center for Best Practices, Council of Chief State School Officers, *Common Core State Standards, Standards for English Language Arts and Literacy History/Social Studies, Science and Technical Studies* (National Governors Association Center for Best Practices, Council of Chief State School Officers: Washington D.C., 2010).

An excellent Catholic school provides programs and services aligned with the mission to enrich the academic program and support the development of student and family life.[12]

If resiliency is the ability to bounce back from failure, what should be done about the parents who refuse to allow their children to fail? If they forget their homework or their lunch, or fail to understand a homework assignment, overprotective parents who are eager to see their children shine at all costs are faced with a dilemma. Author Paul Tough, in his book *How Children Succeed*,[13] encourages us, backed by solid research, to see the benefits of allowing children to fail in small ways as part of the road to success in adulthood.

*Finding 7:* Many attackers felt bullied, persecuted or injured by others prior to the attack.

The National Threat Assessment Center provides strong research to support the need to foster a culture of respect and strong bonding between adults and students as the primary prevention of school violence.[14] The recommendations all fully align with VBRD™. The major components and tasks for creating a safe school climate include:

- Assessment of the school's emotional climate.

- Emphasis on the importance of listening in schools.

---

12. *National Standards and Benchmarks for Effective Catholic Elementary and Secondary Schools,* Center for Catholic School Effectiveness, School of Education, Loyola University Chicago, in partnership with Roche Center for Catholic Education, School of Education, Boston College (2012).

13. Paul Tough, *How Children Succeed: Grit, Power and the Hidden Power of Character* (Boston: Houghton Mifflin Harcourt, 2012).

14. Robert A. Fein, Ph.D., Bryan Vossekuil, William S. Pollack, Ph.D., Randy Borum, Psy.D., William Modzeleski, and Marisa Reddy, Ph.D., *Threat Assessment in Schools: A Guide to Managing Threatening Situations and to Creating Safe School Climates* (Washington, D.C.: United States Secret Service and United States Department of Education, 2002).

- Adoption of a strong but caring stance against the code of silence.

- Prevention of, and intervention in, bullying.

- Involvement of all members of the school community in planning, creating and sustaining a school culture of safety and respect.

- Development of trusting relationships between each student and at least one adult at school.

- Creation of mechanisms for developing and sustaining safe school climates.

The year 2012 was punctuated by two significant acts of violence: one in a movie theatre in Aurora, Colorado, and the other in an elementary school in Newtown, Connecticut. The shock waves that resulted from these events have been driving discussions about mental health, gun safety, and building security. Another emerging theme is the brain research to more fully understand the phenomena of murder-suicides. Andrew Solomon, author of *Far From the Tree: Parents, Children and the Search for Identity,* referenced the work of psychiatrist Dr. Karl Menninger in a *New York Times* article. He noted that suicide is coincidental with the wish to kill, to be killed, and to die. Solomon further states in his commentary on the Newtown, Connecticut shooting:

> But to understand a murder-suicide, one has to start with the suicide, because that is the engine of such acts. Adam Lanza committed an act of hatred, but it seems that the person he hated the most was himself. If we want to stem violence, we need to begin by stemming despair.[15]

In the first half of 2011, there were 313 murder-suicide events that resulted in 313 suicides and 378 homicides.[16] This is clearly a reason

---

15. *Anatomy of a Murder-Suicide*, Andrew Solomon, *The New York Times* opinion page, December 22, 2012

16. *American Roulette: Murder-Suicide in the United States,* fourth edition (Washington, D.C.: Violence Policy Center, 2012)

to fortify our children with the virtue of hope, which offsets despair. There is an article, *"Virtue Can Aid Us With Violence,"*[17] included in the appendix that may be useful to reprint in your community. Recognizing the painful misjudgments that cause such tragic deaths can be a way to help children understand the hand of God as an instrument of healing, and as the source of the cardinal virtues of faith, hope, and love.

In more recent years, school violence has moved to college campuses. Is it possible that we failed to understand or fully address school violence in our elementary and high schools, and that these students carried their pain into early adulthood without healthy resolution? One idea that resonates is the notion that we never give away more pain than we hold in our hearts. Just imagine the anguish of these young attackers who spend their human energy creating such tragic events. Because stories provide us with a way to organize our thinking, we are able to begin such a process as we read these important documents.

The U.S. Secret Service joined the U.S. Department of Education and the Federal Bureau of Investigation releasing a joint report in April 2010 called *Campus Attacks: Targeted Violence Affecting Institutions of Higher Education.* The goal of this report was to review 272 incidents of violence that affected institutions of higher education in the United States from 1900 through 2008. The researchers explored fundamental questions surrounding these events concerning offenders, their connection to those institutions and other relevant factors. The report cites the top two reasons for the violent attacks:

1.  Related to Intimate Relationships

2.  Retaliation for Specific Actions

This speaks to the unquestionable need for healthy communication and conflict resolution skills. Upon hearing of the numerous reports of

---

17. "Virtue Can Aid Us With Violence," by Lynne Lang, appendix 8

young people staging attacks on college campuses,[18] we should have a greater sense of urgency to work with younger children in cultivating a loving school environment.

In 2010, Archbishop Robert J. Carlson, archbishop of Saint Louis, announced a groundbreaking Mission Advancement Initiative to support Catholic education called *Alive In Christ!* The campaign identified academic excellence, evangelization and Catholic identity, and stewardship as key ingredients to revitalizing Catholic education. It became evident that VBRD™ has a central role in supporting this effort.[19] Modeling a life of virtue, treating others with dignity, working to fully express the shared school mission, and nurturing a safe learning environment through restorative practices are essential ingredients for an evangelizing school. These are the hallmarks of VBRD™.

School climate is seen as the foundation and capstone of school success. It begins with the initial contact in a school and ends with the last step outside the building. It is a dynamic experience, depending on the people and circumstances one comes in contact with. Even though we all have days when we are not at our best, in schools there is a prevailing culture that exists in the charism of the leadership and the overall beliefs in the hearts of all in the building. So, kindhearted teachers with high expectations can motivate children to high levels of success.

In a focus group session, a principal once said: "It is easy to have impressive bulletin boards, nice liturgies, rosaries, slogans, and good academic programs, but the true Catholic identity is what is in our hearts. If we don't believe, live, and embrace our Catholic faith, these other things mean nothing. VBRD™ gives us a way to do this with practical tools, and we are working with parents for a consistent message about faith and discipline."

---

18. Diana A. Drysdale, William Modzeleski and Andre B. Simons, *Campus Attacks: Targeted Violence Affecting Institutions of Higher Education* (Washington, D.C.: U.S. Secret Service, U.S. Department of Education and Federal Bureau of Investigation, 2010).

19. *The Role of School Climate in Mission Advancement*, by Lynne Lang (see www.virtuebase.org).

# CHAPTER 3

## LAYING A SPIRITUAL
## FOUNDATION OF VIRTUE

*"When you encounter difficulties and contradictions, do not try
to break them, but bend them with gentleness and time."*

Saint Francis de Sales

BY SECULAR DEFINITION, virtues are core characteristics valued by moral philosophers and religious thinkers. Virtue predates Christianity by several hundred years, which is important in our understanding of its influence on cultures throughout history. The most influential thinking on virtue by philosophers can be found in China, Southern Asia, and the West. These are the civilizations we hear recorded most in history regarding philosophy and religions. Some cultures do not accept what is taught in Judeo-Christian virtue regarding supernatural forces. Popular thought on virtue more easily accepts secular and rational aspects of human existence. In this book, we will emphasize the foundation of virtue necessary for implementation of VBRD™.

Natural virtues in non-Christian belief systems challenge their followers to be good for the sake of goodness. There are many parallels to the virtues outlined by Plato and Socrates in the fifth century BC; however, they were rooted in civic responsibility according to the order of the society at that time. Some non-Christian cultures embrace virtue within the context of other religious deities, such as Tao (The Way) and Buddha (Enlightened One).[20]

One of the most comprehensive publications in this field of study, *Character Strengths and Virtues: A Handbook and Classification*, provides not only a classification system for a multitude of character traits and virtues, but also looks at measures of success in achieving them. The authors, Christopher Peterson and Martin Seligman, have compiled an invaluable resource for reference in this field of study.

With the great variety of philosophies surrounding virtue, these concepts can be widely accepted to meet criteria within any given context of shared values and beliefs. Because of the popularity of the Character Education movement as a common denominator for what we can agree to in maintaining order and civility with schools, many wonder why we don't hear more about it in Catholic schools.

The distinction between the current Character Education movement and the virtue base of VBRD™ is that Catholic virtues are not equal to character traits. As children file into classrooms ready to begin a new school year, teachers in classrooms across the United States and beyond create lists and charts that state such things as: We will keep our hands and feet to ourselves; we will not destroy the property of others; we will not talk out of turn; etc. We teach the expected behavior within any given social context. If we are in public, we have certain behaviors we are expected to display in various settings. Libraries are quiet; symphonies or theater performances require applause at certain times and quiet at others. These are expectations that create order and civility. Social context requires such things as honesty and fairness, but external forces drive these traits. In VBRD™, within the context of Catholic identity, we approach this model just as Scripture teaches: "But seek first his kingdom and his righteousness, and all these things shall be yours as well" (Mt 6:33).

---

20. Christopher Peterson and Martin Seligman, *Character Strengths and Virtues: A Handbook and Classification* (New York: Oxford University Press, 2004), pp. 40-55.

This means that cultivating virtue must be "an inside job" that begins with prayer, seeking the supernatural experience while living in the natural world. Prayerfully seeking the encounter with God that transcends our human experience is precisely where implementation begins.

Another distinction outlined by Peterson and Seligman is the fact that there are character strengths that make up virtues.[21] They list six classic virtues most commonly cited by philosophers and religious thinkers and found throughout the history of civilization as essential for human survival: wisdom, courage, humanity, justice, temperance, and transcendence. It is easy to see how these are essential to society, and we see how they celebrate the human experience. There are mile markers along the way to growing these virtues. These are identified as character strengths.

The road to **wisdom** is marked with character traits including a love of learning, curiosity, and creativity. Such traits are identified as milestones along the way to virtue. The cardinal virtue of prudence is connected to wisdom.

**Courage** is identified as fortitude in the cardinal virtues. It entails extraordinary bravery and the ability to accomplish difficult tasks for the greater good.

**Humanity** can be likened to kindness, compassion, empathy, and the theological virtue of love. This is essential to peaceful coexistence.

**Justice** is fairness. It is also identified as a cardinal virtue. This is essential for living out the ideals of social justice when paired with humanity.

**Transcendence** is linked to the theological virtues of faith, hope, and love. It takes into account beauty, creativity, humor (joy), and the belief in something greater than us at work in the world.

**Temperance** is a virtue linked to what many may refer to as self-control. This is the ability to act in moderation, so as to not be driven by passions, or physical desires.

---

21. *Ibid.*, p. 13.

*To implement, must start w/ selves...*

A great deal of time in VBRD™ training is initially spent talking about and exercising the components of spiritual formation, reflection and sharing. The value of living personal virtue as adults is a vital part of implementation. In some cases, as we begin VBRD™ training, we encounter expressions of frustration, such as: "But when are we going to learn how to implement this in our classrooms?" The interior experience of virtue must take precedence; otherwise, this work will take on qualities similar to character education. We are not teaching the virtue base without first living it. This takes into account the whole adult person as a divine creation, separate from the culture of the professional life, which is filled with obligations and responsibilities, and complicated by our human circumstance.

The Golden Rule takes little effort when people around us are nice or when things are going well for us personally. But it seems that as soon as someone hurts us, we spin to Old Testament beliefs that lead us to eye for eye, tooth for tooth. When Jesus was questioned about which commandment was the greatest, his words became embedded in the hearts of those who heard his answer, and the Holy Spirit has continued to transmit that powerful message for more than two thousand years. This commandment, found in *Matthew* 22:37-39, provides a simple, yet profound recipe for deep, abiding joy: "You shall love the Lord your God with all your heart, and with all your soul, and with all your mind. This is the greatest and first commandment. And a second is like it: You shall love your neighbor as yourself."

*Greatest Commandment*

Loving God and loving neighbor can bring us a lifetime of challenges, especially when we consider all the people in our lives we find unlovable at times, including ourselves! If these two commandments seem short and sweet, let's add another one: the Golden Rule. This is also found in our Christian Scriptures and is translated in every other major religion. In fact, many of the philosophies throughout history that embrace virtue without transcendence hold the Golden Rule as central to achieving civility: "So whatever you wish that men would do to you, do so to them" (Mt 7:12).

With this good guidance in our faith, why do we still struggle in our relationships? The answer is simple, according to the *Catechism*: "Sin is present in human history; any attempt to ignore it or to give this dark reality other names would be futile" (No. 386).

Accepting our fallen nature is a reality that all humanity faces. Knowing that sin is present and has been since the fall of man, the *Catechism* goes further to define it:

> To try to understand what sin is, one must first recognize the profound relation of man to God, for only in this relationship is the evil of sin unmasked in its true identity as humanity's rejection of God and opposition to him, even as it continues to weigh heavy on human life and history. (386)

When we think about the need for kindness in a fallen world, as noted previously, consider the divine kindness of God. Just imagine this amazing God who was kind enough to create the world and all that it holds:

> And God said, "Let the earth bring forth living creatures according to their kinds: cattle and creeping things and beasts of the earth according to their kinds." And it was so. And God made the beasts of the earth according to their kinds and the cattle according to their kinds, and everything that creeps upon the ground according to its kind. And God saw that it was good. Then God said, "Let us make man in our image, after our likeness; and let them have dominion over the fish of the sea, and over the birds of the air, and over the cattle, and over all the earth, and over every creeping thing that creeps upon the earth." So God created man in his own image, in the image of God he created him; male and female he created them. And God blessed them, and God said to them, "Be fruitful and multiply, and fill the earth and subdue it; and have dominion over the fish of the sea and over the birds of the air and over every living thing that moves upon the earth." And God said, "Behold, I have given you every plant yielding seed which is upon the face of all the earth, and every tree with seed in its fruit; you shall have them for food. And to every beast of the earth, and to

every bird of the air, and to everything that creeps on the earth, everything that has the breath of life, I have given every green plant for food." And it was so. And God saw everything that he had made, and behold, it was very good. (*Genesis* 1:24-31)

Every single word in Scripture is meaningful. Consider the implications of this passage:

- God created the universe and all it holds, acknowledging its goodness.

- We were created in God's image.

- We are elevated above all of creation; we are "very good."

- We were given authority and a purpose.

- We were given provision.

Here is what the *Catechism* tells us about our existence:

> God, infinitely perfect and blessed in himself, in a plan of sheer goodness freely created man to make him share in his own blessed life. For this reason . . . God draws close to man. He calls man to seek him, to know him, to love him with all his strength. He calls together all men, scattered and divided by sin, into the unity of his family, the Church. To accomplish this . . . God sent his Son as Redeemer and Savior. In his Son and through him, he invites men to become, in the Holy Spirit, his adopted children and thus heirs of his blessed life. (1)

So, the first amazingly kind act was creation. To top that, we were granted access to the fullness of heaven when Jesus died for our human failings. Teaching children one basic fundamental belief could quite possibly renew the virtue of hope in a time when children are taking their own lives at an unprecedented rate. Humans are of immeasurable worth. The intrinsic, inviolable dignity of the human person is the very fiber of existence from the moment of conception until natural death.

This means that the offenses against the human person through bullying and other types of harm cannot diminish our goodness or worth.

This simple fact has been lost in modern culture. We have come to
believe that if something in the natural world attempts to destroy or
diminish our intrinsic goodness, our worth WILL be destroyed. For
instance, if someone calls me a name, or says something hurtful about
my appearance, then I will be damaged by that statement or action.
This is simply not true in the supernatural world, and we fail to believe this and fail to teach it to children. If, in fact, we believed in our
inviolable dignity, we would pay far less attention to the words and
actions of others toward us. We would acknowledge these attempts to
diminish us, but we would be emboldened to refuse to allow these attempts to cause undue anxiety. This is where virtue can be an avenue
for self-care and can positively impact those around us. Our American
government states that we have "inalienable rights to life, liberty, and
the pursuit of happiness." Other governments may state that their citi-
zens have certain rights at birth. This denies our faith teaching: We are
entitled to rights prior to birth.

> In a special way, believers in Christ must defend and pro-
> mote this right, aware as they are of the wonderful truth re-
> called by the Second Vatican Council: 'By his incarnation the
> Son of God has united himself in some fashion with every hu-
> man being.' This saving event reveals to humanity not only the
> boundless love of God who 'so loved the world that he gave his
> only Son' (Jn 3:16), but also the incomparable value of every
> human person.[22]

To expand on this idea of our immeasurable worth, we are further
reminded that Jesus modeled perfect humanity as he awaited his death,
hanging on the cross: "Father, forgive them; for they know not what
they do" (Lk 23:34).

---

22. Pope John Paul II, *Evangelium Vitae,* encyclical letter on the value and inviolabil-
ity of human life (Rome: Libreria Editrice Vaticana, 1995), 2.

His human nature defies our instincts in offering forgiveness to his murderers. If Jesus can do that much, how much less is asked of us daily? We can surrender for the glory of God our daily sufferings: the person who cuts us off in traffic; the coworker who jams the copy machine and leaves it; the sidewiping comment that stings with rudeness or sarcasm. If even a truthful comment is not spoken out of love, then it may not be well received.

Probably one of the most common and most damaging sins to relationships is gossip — the detracting comments that hurt the good names we are born with. Again, referring to the instruction in the *Catechism* regarding the Eighth Commandment, we must consider our responsibility to uphold a high standard if we are to change the hearts and minds of children:

> Respect for the reputation of persons forbids every attitude and word likely to cause them unjust injury. He becomes guilty:
>
> – of rash judgment who, even tacitly, assumes as true, without sufficient foundation, the moral fault of a neighbor;
>
> – of detraction who, without objectively valid reason, discloses another's faults and failings to persons who did not know them;
>
> – of calumny who, by remarks contrary to the truth, harms the reputation of others and gives occasion for false judgments concerning them. (2477)

In our daily interactions with others, it is our challenge to face daily acts of unkindness with wisdom and grace. If we are not prepared with a prayerful heart and clear vision of our heavenly home, we easily fall short and stumble on those large boulders we all face: blame, revenge and pride, to name a few. The only way to counteract these sinful behaviors is by cultivating virtue. Virtues such as humility, meekness, charity, and justice can play a part in changing our thoughts, words and deeds, shaping us for heaven. Once again, we refer to the *Cat-*

*echism*, which cites *Philippians* 4:8 to express the importance of cultivating virtue:

> "Whatever is true, whatever is honorable, whatever is just, whatever is pure, whatever is lovely, whatever is gracious, if there is any excellence, if there is anything worthy of praise, think about these things."

*NT advice*

A virtue is an habitual and firm disposition to do the good. It allows the person not only to perform good acts, but to give the best of himself. The virtuous person tends toward the good with all his sensory and spiritual powers; he pursues the good and chooses it in concrete actions.

The goal of a virtuous life is to become like God. (1803)

Now let's revisit figure 1 again, and add the concept of virtue into the typical behaviors being addressed. See figure 3:

FIGURE 3

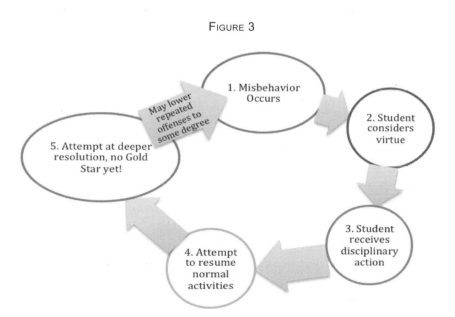

Living a life of virtue is not easy! Think of all the times we are tempted to criticize or judge one another and then act on these thoughts without even realizing what we are doing. Teachers have been observed paying more attention to the "good" students than to the disruptive ones. How often do we remember past offenses and choose to avoid certain individuals or situations? When Jesus walked the earth, he dined with sinners; yet so many times in modern life we gravitate to our friends and close ourselves off from opportunities to stretch our frame of mind regarding others who might not fit our expectations.

If virtue is a habit of holiness, the first order of business in growing it is to pray, asking for God's grace to see what needs to be done — first in oneself. This timeworn expression can be useful in beginning to cultivate a mindset for virtue: "Before you talk to the person about God, talk to God about the person." Prayer for inspiration can be the best way to begin. This book will offer resources for adults at school and adults at home in beginning this discernment process to help determine the best virtue to "assign" to a given situation. By taking time to allow virtue to be illuminated in our own hearts, the world around us will become brighter by our presence and our practices of these good habits. It cannot be stressed enough how important it is to open our spirits to a new way of seeing.

The *Catechism* offers great guidance for learning and praying about virtues (see Nos. 1803-1845). Some people seem to be naturally virtuous, while others may struggle with great crosses such as addiction, poor temperament, or a lackluster character. No matter what our experience or disposition, we are all created for goodness. Some of us simply need to work harder to find it in others, or even harder to cultivate it within ourselves. This good work must begin with our own interior lives before we can expect change from others. The beauty of living a virtuous life is that it cannot exist without a relationship with God. We are created to have that dependency; and the more we work at it, the more intimate it becomes. At the same time, the world around us witnesses the fruit of that relationship by our good works and our holy disposition. As the *Catechism* states:

*virtue a matter of intellect + will*

*(mind)* *(heart/zeal)*

Human virtues are firm attitudes, stable dispositions, habitual perfections of intellect and will that govern our actions, order our passions, and guide our conduct according to reason and faith. They make possible ease, self-mastery and joy in leading a morally good life. The virtuous man is he who freely practices the good.

*human effort is essential*

The moral virtues are acquired by human effort. They are the fruit and seed of morally good acts; they dispose all the powers of the human being for communion with divine love. (1804)

The work of virtue is integral to the restorative discipline process and is the foundation of VBRD.™ For this reason school personnel must lay this groundwork by cultivating personal virtue. Otherwise, nothing else will work. It is my experience that most teachers fall into one of three categories: the No-No's, the So-So's and the Gung-Ho's.

## Oh-No's

These individuals may be heard saying: "Oh-no, there's no need to do things any differently. Oh-no, we don't need to change anything to add more work." These people are minimally performing in their jobs, just going through the motions. They may or may not be checking the help-wanted ads, but they may consider the possibility that they are "misfits" in their current positions.

## So-So's

This script may sound like this: "So, I'm doing a pretty good job. So, I think since things are going well, I'm actually happy with the way things are and don't need to write new lesson plans, try new ideas, or do anything else that might overload me. After all, the pay here is So-So, and I have other things outside of work I enjoy doing, too." These people consider themselves functioning at a pretty good level. They are content with their performance and are not expecting more from themselves because they are getting recognition for being "on track."

## Gung-Ho's

These are people who are constantly looking for new, better, more innovative ways to reach students and to become better people. They greet adversity with enthusiasm and optimism. Generally, they are the go-to people the staff can always count on to help out and pitch in without complaint.

This VBRD™ work will challenge each of these groups. What are you willing to do to improve yourself and the world around you? This book will give you the tools to improve. As one teacher said, "With this work, there are only two groups — those improving and those trying to do so." Those who choose to remain unchanged or refuse to engage in self-reflection and evaluation will eventually resign.

At one of our schools in Saint Louis while working on this process, we had a discussion about the virtue chosen for the coming month: thankfulness. One teacher, deep in thought about her bulletin board, asked, "What is the difference between thanksgiving and thankfulness?" What a great question to consider among the staff at a school still learning this process. The foreword written by Cardinal Raymond Burke for Fr. Joseph F. Classen's book *Meat and Potatoes Catholicism*[23] did not simply state, "Thanks, I hope you write more books." It read, "I hope he will continue his work of pastoral charity begun in this work." The words seem to point to an interior change of disposition. So if I say "thanks for doing that," I am acknowledging what was done, rather than the impact a good act has had on me. "I am thankful for the help" means somehow I have received something deeper. While this may seem like a minor detail, it is genuinely part of the deep-seated impact that virtues can have in a school environment. I have watched it happen.

In much the same way, the tenth leper who returned to thank Jesus for being healed in *Luke* 17:11-19 was clearly transformed and moved, expressing gratitude. While we will never know the ongoing stories of the ten lepers, we do know that one was affected profoundly and perhaps chose to evangelize — sharing the good news of a healer who

---

23. Rev. Joseph F. Classen, *Meat and Potatoes Catholicism* (Huntington, Ind.: Our Sunday Visitor, 2008), p. 17.

changed his life forever. That change became evident to those around him, in turn potentially changing them as well. Virtue begets virtue. Virtue, when cultivated in cooperation with God, changes the natural world. It can be as simple as a bigger smile, or sitting with a suffering friend, or choosing forgiveness. Whatever it is, it springs from the kindness of God who loves us, and our acts are an expression of gratitude to God.

In this same school where one teacher asked about thanksgiving, another teacher reported that one of her students actually included the virtue of seeing God in others in a report about a great historical figure. The teacher knew that this was the fruit of the work she had been doing with her students, and that when virtue is illuminated, it can leave a lasting imprint. It did for both the student and the teacher in this case.

> For this very reason, you should make every effort to sup-
> plement your faith with virtue, and virtue with knowledge, and
> knowledge with self-control, and self-control with steadfastness,
> and steadfastness with godliness, and godliness with brotherly
> affection, and brotherly affection with love. For if these things
> are yours and abound, they keep you from being ineffective or
> unfruitful in the knowledge of our Lord Jesus Christ (2 Peter
> 1:5-8).

In the next chapter, you will learn more about specific virtues by definition and begin to understand the critical role this will play in the successful implementation of this initiative, whether you are a parent or an educator.

# CHAPTER 4

## BECOMING A STUDENT
## OF VIRTUE

*"Love is itself the fulfillment of all our works.*
*There is the goal; that is why we run:*
*we run toward it, and once we reach it,*
*in it we shall find rest."*

Saint Augustine

IF WE CONSIDER WHAT QUALITY could make us more pleasant to live with, most of us would immediately begin working on patience. After all, the expression "patience is a virtue" may well have helped us establish an understanding of what virtue is, by nature of understanding that patience is a worthwhile endeavor. This timeworn expression is believed to have originated in the 1300s with Christian poet William Langland's work *Piers Plowman*. Nearly every school faculty agrees that patience is in short supply as the school year progresses toward summer break. However, by becoming a student of virtue, you will be able to learn about much more than patience with students or family members.

All colors come from any combination of the basic three colors: blue, yellow, and red. For instance, by combining red and yellow in varying amounts, you can achieve a wide range of orange shades, and by combining yellow and blue, you make green, and so on. In the same way, there are basic virtues from which all other virtues flow. Monks in medieval times taught that the fruits of the Spirit in *Galatians* 5:22-23 express the foundational virtues of "love, joy, peace, patience, kindness, goodness, faithfulness, gentleness, self-control; against such there is no law."

Catholics today choosing to study virtue will be encouraged to begin with the foundational cardinal and theological virtues. The *Catechism of the Catholic Church* has an entire section (Part Three, *Life in Christ*) devoted to these "Top Seven," which is a recommended resource in beginning your study of virtue. In addition, Father Benedict Groeschel's *The Virtue Driven Life*[24] devotes a chapter to each of these and provides discussion questions. Become familiar with virtue and learn how it works in the natural world so it can have practical application in your everyday experiences. Once you learn about each specific virtue, it will be easy to identify associated behaviors in very practical ways. Various situations will require different virtues, so it is important to learn as much as possible to develop a large vocabulary of virtue. This will pay off in any circumstance in which we desire to cultivate the good.

The language of Catholic virtues may be challenging to some readers because the virtues are somewhat foreign to our modern-day ears. However, I am reminded of a conversation with Sister Cathy Doherty, a colleague and director of religious education. She inspired the idea that we need to teach even the youngest students the actual names of virtues as identified in the *Catechism*. Her thinking is this: If a small child can say "Tyrannosaurus rex" or "supercalifragilisticexpialidocious," then can we not teach them "prudence" or "temperance"? These words bring children a sense of pride in knowing what they mean and what they can inspire.

> Human virtues acquired by education, by deliberate acts and by a perseverance ever-renewed in repeated efforts are purified and elevated by divine grace. With God's help, they forge

---

24. Father Benedict Groeschel, *The Virtue Driven Life* (Huntington, Ind.: Our Sunday Visitor, 2006).

character and give facility in the practice of the good. The virtuous man is happy to practice them.

It is not easy for man, wounded by sin, to maintain moral balance. Christ's gift of salvation offers us the grace necessary to persevere in the pursuit of the virtues. Everyone should always ask for this grace of light and strength, frequent the sacraments, cooperate with the Holy Spirit, and follow his calls to love what is good and shun evil. (*CCC* 1810-1811)

## THEOLOGICAL VIRTUES

### Faith

Even though faith seems abstract, the truth is, we profess our faith each time we proclaim the Apostles' Creed or the Nicene Creed. Don't get discouraged if you have doubts about your faith. Even the apostles had doubts — this is natural in our human limitations. The expression "Doubting Thomas" comes from the apostle Thomas who claimed he needed to touch the nail marks of the risen Jesus before he could believe. *Hebrews* 11:1 tells us, "Faith is the assurance of things hoped for, the conviction of things not seen." Our faith must rely on surrendering to what lies beyond our human understanding, which is why faith is a supernatural virtue.

### Hope

*Hebrews* 10:23 says, "Let us hold fast the confession of our hope without wavering, for he who promised is faithful." It must be our will to surrender to the hope that our God is loving and faithful. Sadly, we hear frequent reports of suicide and depression, a clear sign of the need to practice the virtue of hope. Praying with confidence against hopelessness can seem insurmountable, but Saint Paul tells us in *Romans* 8:18, "I consider that the sufferings of this present time are not worth comparing with the glory that is to be revealed to us." Hope relies on what is unseen, so our faith is integral to hope.

## Love

Jesus told his apostles, "A new commandment I give to you, that you love one another; even as I have loved you, that you also love one another. (Jn 13:34). Saint Paul states in *1 Corinthians* 13:13, "So faith, hope, love abide, these three; but the greatest of these is love." This is the pure love that is beyond our human capacity, that is supernatural. How many times do we get angry and hold a grudge against another? While anger is not an unhealthy feeling, many times inappropriate actions that result can cause serious harm to those around us. This can result in pain and anxiety for our loved ones at home. If love is the greatest of the cardinal virtues, we must attempt to put the greatest amount of effort into practicing it.

## CARDINAL VIRTUES

Saint Augustine articulated great wisdom regarding these virtues:

> To live well is nothing other than to love God with all one's heart, with all one's soul and with all one's efforts; from this it comes about that love is kept whole and uncorrupted (through temperance). No misfortune can disturb it (and this is fortitude). It obeys only [God] (and this is justice), and is careful in discerning things, so as not to be surprised by deceit or trickery (and this is prudence). (*CCC* 1809)

## Prudence

Avoiding evil, negativity, and foolishness is linked with wisdom. Prudence demands this type of restraint as a way to grow in wisdom. *Proverbs* 14:18 states, "The simple acquire folly: but the prudent are crowned with knowledge." Prudence is having clear thinking and reasoning in any given circumstance so one can choose and act for the good. You may have a person you typically go to for advice — a person who tends to see things with perspective and may even challenge your thinking or your actions. This is the person who may have had helpful experiences and can steer you away from pitfalls when choosing your course of action. This person most likely acts with prudence. Prudence also can be seen in the face of gossip. A person with prudence would not only choose to remain silent, but also might build up the person who is not there to defend himself or herself.

## Temperance

When we were working with a group of middle school students to define this virtue, they could only find information on the Temperance Movement, which began in the 1800s and called for moderation of and even abstaining from alcohol consumption. According to Scripture teaching, however, this moral virtue challenges us to moderation and restraint in our desire for created goods. In *Thessalonians* 5:21, we are encouraged to "hold fast what is good." Perhaps we can easily reflect on times we face temptation and need to practice temperance when we are offered additional servings of food or beverages at a meal, or choose to watch television rather than exercise. Another example of temperance, however, may be in our use of electronic devices. Perhaps using restraint in checking messages or texting a friend would be a good way to practice this virtue.

## Justice

This virtue can inspire us to sit a bit taller in our seats at the thought of being treated with proper and due dignity. In order to act with justice and fairly administer justice, however, prudence must be working in cooperation. If we could focus on basic moral principles that cross the barriers of religions and cultures, we might state that justice recognizes simple truths:

1.  Everyone deserves to be treated with dignity.

2.  Relationships are more important than power or money.

3.  Your behavior in private and public should be the same, obeying only God.                    *seamless garment*

In a school setting, the way a student treats another when no one is around must be consistent with what happens when there are witnesses.

So many times bullying reports cannot be proven, and in these cases it is difficult to act with justice.

Public figures, from businessmen and civic leaders to our presidents, have been involved in scandals that have destroyed their credibility and, in some cases, cost them their positions. Many such instances become part of the fabric of our political history, serving to tarnish the reputations of the individuals and their families and bring scandal to the public positions they hold.

Biblical justice is not the same as legal justice. Acting in fairness, with compassion toward humanity, may result in decisions that appear different in classrooms than in courtrooms. For instance, a teacher may assign a lesser degree of homework to a student who struggles than to a student who is more capable.

The contrast between public life and private life is also evident through social networking. Unfortunately, young people are losing opportunities for college scholarships and jobs as a result of posting inappropriate personal information on Internet sites for public viewing. There is infinite value in living virtuously, always striving for good, so that one's personal life will never be cause for public scandal. From this foundation we can build a process to demonstrate the profound way these beliefs transform everyday experiences into stunning examples of divinity within the human person.

*Micah* 6:8 provides the simplest advice in practicing justice: "and what does the LORD require of you but to do justice, and to love kindness, and to walk humbly with your God?" The moral virtue of justice brings equality and balance; in schools, this is critical to the restorative practices in assuring fair treatment to all parties when harm occurs. Traditional discipline may not provide the opportunity to hear all voices involved, which can result in unjust punishments. God's justice, unlike the justice in the legal system created by humans, relies on the ultimate judgment of what is truly in our hearts — not what we are paid to state, nor in the demands that may have greed as their core intent.

## Fortitude

Courage in the natural world is easy to identify — for example, when a young person chooses to stand up for another child who is being humiliated by others. Virtues are like muscles. The more we exercise them, the stronger they become. Praying for courage draws us closer to God, and the grace we receive strengthens us for the task at hand. When we see circumstances change as a result of our efforts, we are thankful to God. Further graced, we then cultivate other virtues such as thankfulness, hope, and joy.

In addition to learning about these seven virtues from your everyday experiences, also observe the fruit they bear — the result of practicing them. If virtue works for the greater good, then all efforts toward goodness will result in furthering the goal of goodness. For instance, when one chooses to practice fortitude rather than passively watching bullying behavior, the result is justice. The person needing protection may experience relief and perhaps gain a renewed sense of hope. In practicing prudence by choosing to withhold hurtful comments or refusing to participate in gossip, you may feel a surge of grace to experience peace. Perhaps the people you are with choose kind words instead of hurtful ones because of your decision to practice prudence.

Temperance and fortitude are self-regulating virtues designed to  help us control inner desires and strengthen ourselves through moderation. Justice and prudence are for the world of relationships, and they are demonstrated through our actions toward others. The study of virtue provided here is a good start in learning more about these holy habits. Readers are encouraged to investigate further, beginning with those mentioned here. Students can use this chapter for forming ideas and learning the basics about virtue as they plan activities and projects.

Learning practical applications of virtue in the natural world will help in understanding the supernatural encounter with God. For instance, by learning to practice temperance in refraining from a second helping of dessert, we offer that to God as a sacrifice for a need we might have, or for the needs of someone else. We seek God's grace and, in turn, draw closer to him. By observing and practicing virtue in the natural world, we grow closer to Christ and become more holy as we imitate him in our daily walk. As we see the changes around us for the good, we cannot help but respond with gratitude, thereby changing internally in our relationship with God, the giver of all good things. This cycle continues as we are being perfected for heaven. Virtue is a way of life that leads to holiness.

———————————————

The virtues associated with the fruits of the Spirit in *Galatians* 5:22-23 provide a contrast to the seven deadly sins. They present another way of seeing the offsetting actions that are intended to steer us away from destructive habits. These contrasting virtues will provide another layer to the foundation given in the cardinal and theological virtues.

## SEVEN VICES CONTRASTED BY SEVEN VIRTUES

### Pride
Considered the root of all sin (from the beginning of creation), pride is the rejection of God, rebellion against his sovereign authority and a stubbornness of will in accepting his truth. Pride is tamed in our mastery of **humility** (recognizing our need for God). Surrendering our need to be "right" or to blame others for what goes wrong in our lives can open the door for humility.

### Greed
Greed is an inordinate need to accumulate wealth, also referred to as avarice or covetousness. Actively pursuing the virtue of **generosity** can allow one to experience the true joy that comes from this type of charity, or selfless giving. The *Acts of the Apostles* revealed the early Church practices of selling everything and sharing with all in need. This may sound extreme in our modern lives, yet it serves to remind us of the words in *Matthew* 19:21-22: "Jesus said to him, 'If you would be perfect, go, sell what you possess and give to the poor, and you will have treasure in heaven; and come, follow me.' When the young man heard this he went away sorrowful; for he had great possessions."

## Lust

Lust is the desire for physical, sexual pleasures. This vice, when uncontrolled, can cause one to become blind to all else in seeking to gratify one's base desires. Sadly, this blindness can cause distortion in one's understanding of the healthy, holy marital union God calls us to in relating to one another with an openness to life (procreation) and love (God-centered communion with one another as sexual beings). *Humanae Vitae,*[25] the encyclical by Venerable Pope Paul VI that inspired Blessed John Paul II's *Theology of the Body*, addresses this issue. Lust leads to objectification of the body and pornography. It also becomes a gateway to unhealthy sexual pleasures that distort the dignity and nature of human intimacy and brings disorder to relationships. **Chastity** is the virtue that we aspire to in seeking God's will regarding relationships. This is not a popular idea in modern culture, yet the benefits of practicing this virtue enable us to reach self-mastery and liberate us from the desire for selfish, aggressive, or manipulative actions regarding sexual activity. Consider how this virtue can offset the vice. If we could positively influence this one aspect of behavior, we would find a reduction in bullying, which is inextricably linked to domestic and dating violence.

## Anger

Evil and unrighteous attacks against good are at the heart of true bullying behavior. The emotion of anger is acceptable, but the unhealthy expression of it can be sinful. In this context, anger refers to unholy, vengeful, and mean-spirited actions. By practicing **meekness**, we can moderate the disorder created by unhealthy anger; by integrating patience, we can learn to practice forbearance with one another.

## Gluttony

Gluttony is the inordinate, excessive partaking of food and/or drink. This can lead to a desire for pleasures that deny basic provisions for others and cause us to lose our sensibilities and right thinking. The practice of

---

25. Pope Paul VI, *Humanae Vitae,* encyclical letter on the regulation of birth (Rome: Libreria Editrice Vaticana, 1968).

**temperance** moderates our appetites and can lead to better personal health as well as open our minds to consider the best use of all resources, bringing about good stewardship.

## Envy

Envy is sadness over the good fortune of another, as well as joy in the misfortune of another. Envy is distinct and more destructive than jealousy, which wants to solely possess something that belongs to another. With jealousy, one wants to take something for oneself, but with envy, one would rather it be destroyed than watch someone else enjoy it. A good example of this can be found in *Genesis* with Joseph, the favored son, whose brothers were initially jealous of their father's affection for him. This led to envy and their desire to destroy him. But Joseph's unconditional approach of mercy, kindness, and love for them changed their hearts. In this same way, the virtue of **love of neighbor** can transform those around us and heal us of the envy within ourselves.

## Sloth

Sloth is laziness or apathy toward what is good. It can cause one to abandon prayer and good acts, and to slide into passivity, as though life were a television program to be viewed without active engagement. As I think of those children who witness bullying, their unwillingness to step in and support one another may apply here. The offsetting virtue — **courage,** or **fortitude** — can be a powerful antidote for these behaviors.

---

In a booklet published in 2001 by the Knights of Columbus, philosopher Peter Kreeft[26] highlights vices as the opposite of key virtues, and names those opposing the cardinal virtues as folly (pride), injustice, cowardice, and intemperance.

---

26. Peter Kreeft, *Virtues and Vices* (New Haven, CT: Knights of Columbus, 2001).

Kreeft further explains the grave implications, however, for those who reject the three theological virtues. In these actions, eternal salvation is at risk.

## Apostasy

Apostasy is the rejection of Christianity and is a sin against faith. The knowing and deliberate rejection of faith can be demonstrated by neglect, rebellion, or heresy. Those individuals who refuse to practice their Catholic faith and refuse to pass their faith tradition on to their children must be loved (and remember, the greatest virtue is love!) back into the fold in whatever way possible. So the vice of apostasy in another can challenge us to practice the virtue of **faith**, praying for ways to evangelize those who have abandoned the practice of this virtue.

## Despair

The deliberate refusal of hope is despair. Arguably, in today's modern culture, we have a deficit of hope. This is evident by the rising trends in suicide. However, loss of hope cannot be confused with feelings of depression or clinical manifestation of such symptoms. Feelings are not reliable, nor do they demonstrate action. Because we operate out of free will and intellect, we must be freely choosing actions. This requires our full, knowing consent. Despair is not psychological but theological. Kreeft sums up the vices associated with the theological virtues simply: "That is, just as the theological virtues have God as their object — they are three ways of saying yes to God — so their opposites are three ways of saying no to God."[27]

Another aspect of despair is the belief that we can achieve salvation without the cooperation of a relationship with God. If we presume we are on our own, we are rejecting the virtue of **hope** (see also *Catechism*, No. 2092).

## Hate

The vice opposing charity is hate, but it also includes willful actions that lead to hate, such as apathy, spiritual laziness (spiritual sloth), and

---

27. *Ibid.*

ingratitude. We must persevere in virtuous actions to counteract the unforgiveness that causes us to withhold love (charity) toward another. How many times have we held on to resentments or grudges and refused to act lovingly toward another? Deep hurts can bring about fear, thus affecting our ability to fully nurture relationships. The Lord's Prayer can be a great source of healing if we can surrender our need to hold on to bitterness toward others. This decisive act can only happen when we are actively cultivating the virtue of **love**. Christ clearly tells us that if we do not forgive, we cannot be forgiven (see Mt 6:14-15).

---

With the groundwork in virtue here, the path is paved for you, the reader, to begin your journey as a student of virtue. As any good student knows, notebooks and pens are essential. Write down the virtue you are praying about, and log the activity that results from living a virtuous life. It will be an adventure ride like no other when you begin to observe the changes around you and inspire others by your goodness. Mistake-making is part of our human experience. So, when those mistakes begin to cloud your vision for living virtue, be sure to tap in to sacramental grace through every possible avenue. Would you invite a guest into your home without cleaning the kitchen or putting fresh towels in the bathroom? If you knew you were having company, would you clean, straighten, and dust your home? In the same way, our hearts must be straightened and prepared for the most welcomed guest through reception of the Sacrament of Reconciliation and frequent holy Communion. Some of my best writing comes during Adoration before the Blessed Sacrament. So, know that our willingness to listen and reflect is critical to being a good student of virtue. Giving yourself silent time will provide God time for the intimacy that can foster growth.

Virtues are amazing weapons to fight the battle against the vices that plague our human condition. In medieval times, monks were considered the primary teachers of faith and used illustrations to teach. About the year 1300, a manuscript known as *Beinecke MS 416* presented such didactic diagrams from the Cistercian abbey of Kamp in western Germany. Two diagrams, a "Tree of Virtues" and a "Tree of Vices," illustrate the many branches leading from the roots (of all good, and of all evil). The branches and leaves show clusters associated with key behaviors found within each tree.[28] These were a unique surprise in my study of virtue and stand as another example of the varied ways we can come to understand virtue. Becoming a student of virtue can help Catholics learn practical applications of those precepts that seem at times too lofty to understand, much less to aspire to integrate into everyday life.

## How to Grow in Virtue

Peter Kreeft, in his book *Making Choices*,[29] states that in order to make good moral choices, we can use seven "power aids" to deepen our intimacy with the Holy Spirit in seeking to know God's will in our daily experiences in the natural world. It is easy to lose our way, falling into poor habits and making decisions that can negatively affect our relationships with those around us and with God. By using these aids, we can guide ourselves along the right path, confident that we are pleasing God and experiencing peace. The seven are listed here:

### Prayer

Taking time to develop this habit is essential. There are many forms of prayer. So familiarize yourself with them and integrate the habit of prayer if you haven't done so already. It is easy to get too busy to take time to converse with God daily. Be sure it is as important as brushing your teeth.

---

28. "Tree of Virtues" and "Tree of Vices," *Beinecke MS 416*. Beinecke Rare Book and Manuscript Library at Yale University. http://brbl-archive.library.yale.edu/exhibitions/speculum/3v-4r-virtues-and-vices.html
29. Peter Kreeft, *Making Choices: Practical Wisdom for Everyday Moral Decisions* (Cincinnati: Servant Books, 1990), pp. 211-214.

**Familiarity with God's Word**

Take time to read the daily Mass readings or join a Bible study. There is no question on earth that can't be answered in Scripture. Don't be afraid to use a highlighter to underline or otherwise indicate important passages. When I read something that has significance when I am praying with Scripture, I date it and write a few words to remind me of its importance. Sometimes it is nice to look back at what I have written and why it is important. I once had a friend who was ill with cancer, and in her final hours of life, we read her special passages aloud as a comfort to her and as a model of her unshakable faith to all of us gathered around her bedside. That was an unforgettable experience.

**Christian Community**

It cannot be stressed enough how important it is to belong, and VBRD™ offers us an opportunity to strengthen a sense of belonging by the nature of restorative practices and by cultivating holy habits that make us more loving and forgiving with one another.

**Silence**

Our contemplative experiences are meant to draw us closer to God, so that we can become more loving to our neighbors. Some humanistic or religious practices of silence are designed to reach a state of self-hypnosis. Sitting in silence before the Blessed Sacrament, however, allows us to contemplate God's goodness without interruption.

"Joy is not just happiness and satisfaction, but dynamism, movement, strength to win the world. Joy is not just fulfillment, an ending of a quest, but it is power and strength, a beginning."[30]

**Suffering**

This is our willingness to share in the suffering of Christ in both big and small ways, choosing to joyfully sacrifice our will and desire for God's holy will.

---

30. *Ibid.*

**Mary's Example**

As she began her ministry as the mother of Jesus, Mary remained reflective and trusting, and praised God (as expressly stated in the *Magnificat*). Kreeft says she modeled pondering, positivity and praise for us.

―――――――――――――――――――――――

If we are to support one another on the journey to heaven, our efforts will be sustained using these points, and the results will be contagious. As we teach virtue to children, we can plan to simplify the language, but teaching the vocabulary will be just as important for them as it is for us. In order to easily understand virtues, it may be best to keep in mind:

> Put on then, as God's chosen ones, holy and beloved, compassion, kindness, lowliness, meekness and patience, forbearing one another and, if one has a complaint against another, forgiving each other; as the Lord has forgiven you, so you also must forgive. And above all these put on love, which binds everything together in perfect harmony. And let the peace of Christ rule in your hearts, to which indeed you were called in the one body. And be thankful. (*Colossians* 3:12-15)

**Virtues**

- Compassion

- Kindness

- Humility

- Gentleness

- Patience

- Forbearance

- Forgiveness

- Love

- Peace

- Unity

- Thankfulness

Most people can relate to the majority of these virtues, and just reading them can remind us that the Body of Christ is truly beautiful. This Scripture has been a catalyst for incredible change among the students of virtue seeking ways to bring VBRD™ into their communities.

Each time there is a conflict, as you prayerfully discern how to handle it, virtue enters in. It will become second nature to begin your conversation by stating the virtues you are choosing to practice in solving the problem. It is not uncommon to actually write down all the virtues individuals wish to demonstrate in a circumstance. Then, as the conversation begins, there will be a visible sign of what everyone agreed on. If there is disagreement and tension, it is easy to refer back to the agreement to make sure everyone is still on track.

Try the ideas and virtues in this chapter, and keep track of your progress. You will be surprised at the hunger all around you for the virtue of kindness. It doesn't take much to inspire others. So, begin today!

# CHAPTER 5

## HISTORY OF RESTORATIVE PRACTICES

*"This common prayer, the Lord's Prayer, recognizes our
failures and offenses, and acknowledges our dependence
on God's love and mercy."*

U.S. Conference of Catholic Bishops[31]

WHAT CAN BE MORE TROUBLING than feeling unredeemed? Have you
ever made a mistake, only to discover that no matter what you did, you
were not forgiven for your failure? Perhaps you damaged or destroyed
something that you could not easily fix or replace. Or you regrettably
said something hurtful that was held against you without regard for
your remorse. To add insult to injury, the incident may have become
widespread knowledge, and you may have had no way to clear your
name. In such instances, we may desperately attempt to make amends,
but eventually realize we cannot change a hardened heart. In our society, we are losing our ability to resolve conflict face-to-face thanks
to advancing technology. It is creating new, less direct avenues for

---

31. U.S. Conference of Catholic Bishops, *Responsibility, Rehabilitation and Restoration: A Catholic Perspective on Crime and Criminal Justice* (Washington, D.C.:
USCCB, 2000).

communication. A parent commented that she spends a great deal of time with her small children at playgrounds and other such areas, only to notice that while the children are playing, their parents are texting, tweeting, and talking on their cell phones. It is becoming more and more challenging to stay present to those around us without becoming distracted by technology. This is significantly affecting our ability to speak and listen effectively.

In training sessions, I often ask how many have chosen to avoid a person because of something they had heard about that person that detracted from their good name. When many nod in agreement, I further ask if anyone was bold enough to discover more about that person, only to find that a truly good person had been damaged by gossip and rumors. Then stories unfold of heartbreaking events that caused people to feel marginalized, sometimes for the entirety of their childhood and beyond. These low-level incidents offer significant opportunities to demonstrate redemption and can serve to reduce and prevent more serious offenses. Findings mentioned earlier regarding the National Threat Assessment Center indicate that schools intervening early and often in low-level aggression are far less likely to encounter more serious violence:

> Cultures and climates of safety, respect, and emotional support can help diminish the possibility of targeted violence in schools. Environments in which students, teachers, and administrators pay attention to students' social and emotional needs — as well as their academic needs — will have fewer situations that require formal threat assessments.[32]

*Restorative Practices* is a social science that studies how to build social capital and achieve social discipline through collaborative learning

---

32. Robert A. Fein, Ph.D., Bryan Vossekuil, William S. Pollack, Ph.D., Randy Borum, Psy.D., William Modzeleski, and Marisa Reddy, Ph.D., *Threat Assessment in Schools: A Guide to Managing Threatening Situations and to Creating Safe School Climates* (United States Secret Service and United States Department of Education: Washington, D.C., 2002), p. 13.

and decision-making. The International Institute for Restorative Practices (IIRP) began its work with juvenile delinquency and at-risk youth as part of a community partnership in 1977 and expanded its mission in the 1990s. The use of restorative practices helps:

- reduce crime, violence and bullying;

- improve human behavior;

- strengthen civil society;

- provide effective leadership;

- restore relationships;

- repair harm.[33]

Restorative practices offer the hope of worldwide civility and ways to positively impact relationships. In the early work of the IIRP, Pennsylvania schools celebrated a significant reduction in bullying at one school identified as "persistently violent." These practices also set the tone for respectful interactions among students as part of the primary prevention of violence. The Web site gives more information on this promising work, citing specific research on the topic.

While this guide is intended to address harmful behaviors we encounter in our Catholic schools, restorative practices informally took shape within indigenous tribes long before there were systems of institutionalized education. Forms of these practices span many cultures and time periods throughout history. "The moral force of the group was used to persuade people to put the group's good above individual welfare. It is said of a wrongdoer that 'he acts as if he had no relations.'"[34] This referred to the fact that a person had become so disconnected from the community that he had no idea about the impact of his actions.

33. International Institute for Restorative Practices, "What Is Restorative Practices?" http://www.iirp.edu/what-is-restorative-practices.php.
34. Robert Yazzi and James W. Zion, "Navajo Restorative Justice: The Law of Equality and Justice," in *Restorative Justice: International Perspectives*, edited by R. Galaway and J. Hudson (Monsey, NY: Criminal Justice Press), pp. 157-174.

This rings true even more today. Our society is more mobile, families are broken, we struggle to balance the busy pace of careers and activities, and we have new technology. We are more disconnected than at any other time in history. Children today have less time with the significant adults in their lives than ever before. At the same time, they have more access to possessions, information that may or may not be age-appropriate, and more unsupervised time and disposable income. The notion of offending relatives or dishonoring the family name was a deterrent to committing any harmful acts that would affect the Navajo tribe. The solution to these types of occurrences was to sit in a circle with the tribe and talk about what needed to be done to make things right. This reconnecting was known as "peacemaking."

While the twentieth century may not have been the most violent time in human history, it certainly had its share of mass atrocities. The Holocaust of World War II, apartheid in South Africa, and the Rwandan genocide in the 1990s are a few of the indescribably painful events the world witnessed. How can nations recover from mass genocides or government-sanctioned murders? Researcher Dr. Martha Minow studied human rights violations globally in her published work in 1998.[35] There is a delicate balance between moving forward from what happened and relentlessly ruminating over events of the past. Isn't that true for all of us?

The phrase "forgive and forget" has caused a significant amount of pain, particularly for those who have suffered immensely at the hands of others, as in ongoing, severe abuse. The definition of true forgiveness is the ability to untangle ourselves emotionally from the transgressor and the transgression without negatively impacting future relationships. Forgiveness does not come from forgetting, but rather from remembering and surrendering our burdens to Christ, who tells us, "Take my yoke upon you, and learn from me; for I am gentle and lowly in heart, and you will find rest for your souls. For my yoke is easy, and my burden is light" (Mt 11:30).

---

35. Martha Minow, *Between Vengeance and Forgiveness: Facing History after Genocide and Mass Violence* (Boston: Beacon Press, 1998), p. 2.

Finding ways to recover from the effects of these most unimaginable violations against human rights has led to restorative practices. When schools administer compassionate justice, this can create an environment that values making things as right as possible for those experiencing mistreatment.

One of the most significant and promising practices began in South Africa when the Truth and Reconciliation Commission was formed in 1996 after abolishing its death sentence a year earlier.[36] As a response to apartheid, the commission provided a blend of formal investigation, victim testimony, reparation processes, and a mechanism for granting amnesty for perpetrators who honestly reported their role in the violence. This formalized process took shape after more than 30 years of human rights abuses, during which time Archbishop Desmond Tutu received the Nobel Peace Prize for his significant contribution to upholding human dignity.[37] This offered evidence that has shaped a strong foundation for the restorative justice movement.

The Truth and Reconciliation Commission and the Navajo nation both share this idea of telling your story. Because stories help us organize ideas, the value of this process brings a deeper understanding of any situation and is among the best practices in teaching empathy. When we think of storytelling within the context of our faith, the parables of Jesus stand as powerful images that define Christian behavior. This is an age-old concept that has not lost its effectiveness in transferring both history and wisdom.

These large global events that have challenged us to examine our role in peace and justice, along with restorative work within the United States, have initiated changes in the criminal justice system. The restorative justice movement began as it became apparent that the anguish of criminals and their victims could be reduced. The circle process provided a way for each person to express his or her experiences, tell his or her story, repair the harm and restore relationships as much as possible.

---

36. Dennis Sullivan and Larry Tifft, *The Handbook of Restorative Justice: A Global Perspective* (London: Routledge/Taylor and Francis Group, 2006), p. 161.

37. Peter Storey, "A Different Kind of Justice: Truth and Reconciliation in South Africa," *Christian Century*, September 10-17, 1997.

Society reaped the benefits of lower recidivism rates, and reintegration in to society became possible.[38] Criminals were able to find a way to return to productive places in communities after serving their sentences and taking extra steps to restore relationships and repair harm to people and their property. So what are circle processes, and how do they work to make this happen?

The circle process is what we describe as the foundation of the restorative process. Learning to communicate — talk and listen — within a structure that provides a way for mediation occurs as people sit in a circle. All parties are interviewed individually in advance to clarify desires, goals, and expectations. If conditions are right, and the parties agree to attempt to resolve issues collectively, they come together, each with allies (family members, friends, counselors, colleagues, etc.) and trained mediators. Historically, trained mediators are able to help lay the groundwork for a safe and productive process that leads to satisfaction of each person's desires, goals, and expectations.

Church leaders of all faiths have been in strong support of restorative justice work, because it truly expresses the spirit of love and forgiveness. In particular, we embrace these teachings as Catholics and as Christians. Involvement in social justice efforts has been a long-standing role of the U.S. Conference of Catholic Bishops (USCCB). Evidence of this is noted in their pastoral statement, *Responsibility, Rehabilitation and Restoration: A Catholic Perspective on Crime and Criminal Justice*:

> Just as God never abandons us, so too we must be in covenant with one another. We are all sinners, and our response to sin and failure should not be abandonment and despair, but rather justice, contrition, reparation, and return, or re-integration, of all into the community.

On the USCCB Web site there is a section dedicated to restorative justice, which opens with this quote from Pope John Paul II in 2000:

---

38. Jeff Latimer, Craig Dowden, and Danielle Muise, "The Effectiveness of Restorative Justice Practices: A Meta-Analysis," *The Prison Journal*, 85:2 (June 2005): 127-144.

We are still a long way from the time when our conscience can be certain of having done everything possible to prevent crime and to control it effectively so that it no longer does harm and, at the same time, to offer to those who commit crimes a way of redeeming themselves and making a positive return to society. If all those in some way involved in the problem tried to . . . develop this line of thought, perhaps humanity as a whole could take a great step forward in creating a more serene and peaceful society.

## RESTORATION WITHIN CATHOLIC SCHOOLS

While efforts toward a peaceful world seem compelling globally, our work must begin with the smallest efforts toward justice, resolving day-to-day conflicts that effectively teach children about forgiveness. The cycle of pain, rage, and revenge can easily be broken with forgiveness if it relates to a small matter and adults virtuously teach faith-based skills as part of the process. But first, relationships and a reserve of trust must be established. At the heart of restorative practices are talking circles, which are designed to provide emotional safety. The circle "community" has ownership in what happens to its members. This is where stories are told, emotions are expressed, and relationships are healed. This is where harm to people and property can begin to be repaired.

Emotional safety is a key ingredient to violence prevention. When our joy, or positive emotion, is interrupted, then our emotional safety is compromised. The results of this can be predictably unhealthy both for the individual and for society. My early work in curriculum development was based on the work of such pioneers in the field of emotional intelligence as Daniel Goleman[39] and his colleagues. I developed curricula that focused on teaching life skills in communication, problem-solving, critical- and creative-thinking skills, and managing emotions.

---

39. Daniel Goleman, *Emotional Intelligence: Why It Can Matter More Than IQ* (New York: Bantam Books, 1994).

This work quickly became popular because it provided practical skills for middle school students. The lessons were interactive and could be developed more deeply with practice over time. So prior to the work in bullying, these concepts were already part of the primary prevention message. Themes included: self-awareness, critical thinking, verbal and nonverbal communication skills, conflict styles and management, establishing a personal mission statement, and goal setting.

When I discovered the work of Jane Bluestein, Ph.D., in her book *Creating Emotionally Safe Schools*,[40] I became familiar with how emotional safety impacts learning and behavior. When children are exposed to violence of any kind, the window to learning closes — for an undetermined amount of time. By acknowledging the feelings children are experiencing, we can discover and meet their needs. This enables us to help them to return to a place of trust and hope. Talking circles are a valuable tool for optimizing the development of emotional intelligence and assuring emotional safety. The simplest definition of emotional safety comes from Christina Mattise, and elementary school guidance counselor, quoted by Bluestein: "I have the right to learn without having my head, or my heart, or my body, hurt."

When talking circles follow the guidelines provided by experts, they create what I believe to be a supernatural space for operating at a higher frequency. They are a vehicle for cultivating virtue and making important decisions for the good of the community, both within the classroom and beyond. They are sacred. Many times teachers fail to see the benefits of this sacred time and space until there is a serious problem or event. It is in these times that there is a need to draw from the emotional reserve built on the investment of time and effort. For this reason, circles must become routine practice, and not used simply when there is a problem. They can be used to celebrate, collaborate, and problem-solve as a means to building and sustaining a sense of safety and community.

A circle is a versatile restorative practice that can be used proactively, to develop relationships and build community; or

---

40. Jane Bluestein, *Creating Emotionally Safe Schools: A Guide for Educators and Parents* (Deerfield Beach, FL: Health Communications Inc., 2001).

reactively, to respond to wrongdoing, conflicts, and problems Circles give people an opportunity to speak and listen to one another in an atmosphere of safety, decorum, and equality. The circle process allows people to tell their stories and offer their own perspectives. (Pranis, 2005)[41]

The use of informal restorative practices dramatically reduces the need for more time-consuming formal restorative practices. Systematic use of informal restorative practices has a cumulative impact and creates what might be described as a restorative milieu — an environment that consistently fosters awareness, empathy, and responsibility in a way that is likely to prove far more effective in achieving social discipline than our current reliance on punishment and sanctions.[42]

The field of restorative practices provides the framework within which healing and restoration occurs. Readers can learn more about these concepts by visiting the International Institute for Restorative Practices Web site at www.iirp.edu. Several key principles are central to this effort:

- The collaborative leadership model best responds to the needs of all within the group. The fundamental unifying hypothesis of restorative practices is that "human beings are happier, more cooperative and productive, and more likely to make positive changes in their behavior when those in positions of authority do things with them, rather than to them or for them."

- There are three primary stakeholders: those harmed, those causing the harm, and their respective communities of care. (This can

---

41. Kay Pranis, *The Little Book of Circle Processes* (Intercourse, PA: Good Books, 2005).

42. Ted Wachtel, "The Next Step: Developing Restorative Communities." Paper presented at the International Institute for Restorative Practices' Seventh International Conference on Conferencing, Circles, and other Restorative Practices, November 9-11, 2005, Manchester, England.

easily replace the bullying terms referred to in chapter 2: bullies, victims, and bystanders; or as SuEllen Fried and I named them: bulliers, targets, and witnesses.) The very process of interacting is critical to meeting stakeholders' emotional needs. The emotional exchange necessary for meeting the needs of all those directly affected cannot occur with only one set of stakeholders participating.[43]

- There are both formal and informal ways to integrate the processes, and all involve affective communication that offers the ability to speak and listen. This can be as simple as asking questions that challenge thinking and behavior, or as formal as family restorative conferences.

- In restoration, relationships are key, and healthy relationships rely on the free expression of human emotion. By understanding the full range of these emotions, we can increase our capacity for healthy interactions, minimizing negative ones and maximizing our expression of the positive. This work was developed by Silvan S. Tomkins in his research in the psychology of "affect." He developed a scale of nine emotions: Enjoyment, Interest, Surprise, Shame, Distress, Disgust, Fear, Anger, and Dissmell (a reaction to noxious odors). In restorative work, circles and conferencing are structured to create safe places for expression of the full range in order to effectively restore damaged relationships.

- When healthy, positive emotion is interrupted, we experience shame, according to the study of affect by Tomkins.[44] This can trigger unhealthy expressions of emotion. The research of Donald Nathanson[45] has provided insight that can steer victims of crime

---

43. Ted Wachtel and Paul McCold, "In Pursuit of Paradigm: A Theory of Restorative Justice." Paper presented at the XIII World Congress of Criminology, August 10-15, 2003, Rio de Janeiro, Brazil.

44. Silvan S. Tomkins, "Shame," in Donald L. Nathanson (ed.), *The Many Faces of Shame* (New York: Norton), pp. 133-161.

45. Donald L. Nathanson, "Affect Theory and the Compass of Shame," in Melvin Lansky and Andrew Morrison (eds.), *The Widening Scope of Shame* (London: Routledge/Taylor and Francis Group, 2006).

from the cycle of guilt that might plague them. (NOTE: This is a key ingredient to ending the cycle of pain, rage, and revenge that leads to bullying. Our faith teaches us forgiveness, and the Sacrament of Reconciliation can offer the grace to transform our shame into something more useful — being witnesses of the Kingdom on earth.)

- If we believe we are treated fairly, with justice, we do not necessarily need to agree with the outcome. Having a voice in the outcome and having choices can empower all parties and teach children about dignity. If Jesus works with us, in us, and through us, we can model the same for those around us.

As we lay the foundation for the spiritual aspects of disciplining children, let's consider the fact that the word "discipline" is a derivative of the word "disciple." It refers to one's ability to conform or adapt to a desired goal. For our purposes in this work, we are hoping to provide a formative framework in which young people adapt to a life of virtue, thereby turning away from behavior that is not rooted in goodness.

The word "restorative" is to make new, or return to an original state. So, let's think about how many times we are hurt by others and we want things to return to their original condition of goodness, or order. We want an apology, or we want what was broken to be fixed. What about the times we hold in our hearts? Perhaps we wish we could have apologized after screaming at a child, or to one whom we issued an unjust or overly harsh punishment? We know by the look on a child's face that we have crushed a spirit. We feel too overcome with emotion to stop in our tracks and make it right.

The same is true for children. When they cross the line and enter into the territory of unacceptable behavior toward a peer, nine times out of ten they know they are heading down the wrong path. If no one stops the action, it can escalate. We need to give children a way to return to goodness without shaming them. That is the goal of restorative discipline. It seeks to repair harm to relationships caused by unkind behaviors. These behaviors do not necessarily have to be labeled as bullying.

If a fifth-grader carrying balls from the playground pushes a third-grader she may not typically have contact with during a school day, it is not necessarily bullying. It is an unkind, aggressive act. But the more important focus must be to understand the root of her behavior. Would we not do the same for a person experiencing headaches? Rather than simply supplying medication, we must investigate the cause of the headache to ensure that there is not a more serious problem. A threatening diagnosis is a game-changer in the way we see the symptoms. So, too, with a child who suffers another "ailment" that may manifest itself in misbehavior. Virtues of compassion and empathy are critically important in such cases. Should we accept the hurtful behavior? No, but we will hold the child accountable and responsible with this in mind.

Restorative discipline is much more helpful when looking at the overall behaviors in schools that need to be redirected. It deals with potential harm, which is a more appropriate focus than that of "bullying." The bullying label should now be sent out to pasture, because it is a label that locks children into stereotypes that cannot be shaken. "He's a bully" or "She's bullying me" are typical statements that are not always accurate. However, a statement about being "harmed" or experiencing mistreatment is specific to what actually happened and does not require a special definition to categorize the behavior for disciplinary action.

Many people use the word "bullying" loosely and do not always have a good, working definition. But VBRD™ will not need one because it addresses harm, the harmer, and the witnesses. Now, the initial illustration described earlier (figure 1) looks more complete when seeing the fully integrated model in figure 4 on the next page.

This model has proven successful in changing behaviors. The student with the opportunity to choose to practice a virtue is now choosing the relevant consequence and is prayerfully cultivating virtue and modeling what it means to be a Christian. The act of forgiveness and reconciliation reduces the likelihood of further disciplinary actions because it integrates the virtue of justice. Here's an example of the way it works:

**Situation:** Student A talks back to the lunchroom supervisor.

FIGURE 4

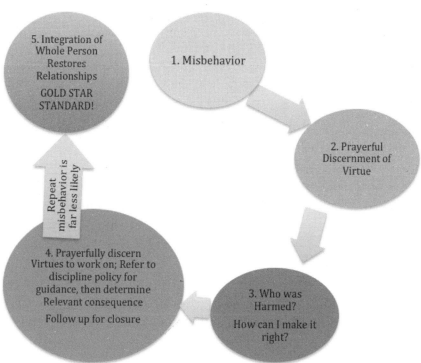

**Consequence in an old model:** Student gets a "check" or demerit.

**Consequence in a restorative model:** The student, supervisor, and another adult meet, pray, identify a virtue they each want to model, discuss the harm, and decide how to repair it. The student decides to apologize and help in the lunchroom for two lunch periods. A closing prayer and a check-in after the two lunch periods brings closure for the supervisor and student.

**Conclusion:** The student reports a deeper appreciation of the supervisor's experience. The supervisor expresses a deeper appreciation for the change of heart. Both have cultivated virtue, and empathy brings forgiveness. Both parties have high accountability and high responsibility to the relationship.

By building empathy with all parties, we teach both adults and students that the cycle of harmful behavior is an act of social injustice. Therefore, until things are made right, we are considering all the ways we need to seek justice in unhealthy ways. Revenge, paybacks, resentment, and unforgiveness plague our litigious society. In the adult world, we want to bring legal action against others who offend us. Children have come by their antisocial behaviors honestly — they have learned them from us! Their world is simply a mirror of ours. Many times, parents seek justice for their child at school. Yet, if they were to examine their own behavior, they might realize there are lessons for everyone in building virtue — beginning with themselves.

This model of virtue and restoration will bring parents and other adults into a deeper understanding of the way we see our world and hold them highly accountable and responsible for proper discipleship of children. A firm adult foundation must be in place long before implementing VBRD™ fully. The catechesis of our Catholic faith can seem complex and academic, but this model provides Church teaching in everyday language and in the human experience.

Do we want to see the misbehavior of children as a punishment waiting to happen? Or, do we want to prayerfully discern ways to grow virtue within ourselves and teach these virtues to children? A hungry world awaits the "soul food" of a virtuous life to bring healing and hope to relationships every single day! It is in our commitment to being constructive and prayerful in thoughts, words, and deeds that we can bring this to fruition. Let's consider scenarios that typify what schools encounter frequently, if not daily:

### Scenario A

Robin gets into trouble for pushing Terese on the playground. Terese tells others that Robin is a "bully." You know that it was an isolated incident and that Robin has had struggles at home. So, you want to give this child a break. But, you can't because other parents are storming your office, outraged that you are doing nothing to stop bullying in your school.

### Scenario B

Chesney has a behavior-disorder diagnosis and is lacking appropriate social cues. He kicks the students in his class during recess and is repeatedly disruptive in the classroom. You are flooded with phone calls by angry parents, insisting that this bully be removed from your school. After all, they all pay tuition, and want their school to be peaceful. He just doesn't fit the picture of a child of God according to the school's standards.

## Scenario C

Your school has very little physical bullying, yet you are certain things could be better. The biggest problems you face are exclusion and verbal assaults suffered by some students, and a sense of entitlement in those students with very involved parents. You don't really have a bullying problem, but everyone wants to classify every act of aggression as bullying when the true problem is simply rudeness.

## Scenario D

Your school demographic is low-income, single-parent families, with a variety of ethnic and cultural backgrounds, and perhaps some cases of domestic violence. Your students lack some basic manners and skills to interact appropriately. As a result, children can be rude and dismissive of one another. You don't consider this bullying, but rather a need for awareness and education in social skills.

If these sound familiar, then many attempts at implementing anti-bullying or bullying prevention programs may not be the answer to your challenges. In the pages ahead, you will learn the step-by-step process of changing your school climate — one incident, one child, one parent, one teacher, and one volunteer at a time. The Kingdom wasn't built in a day. So, allow three years to see extensive fruit from this labor of divine love. This book was written to share the immediate, short-term successes that, over time, will yield more devout, faith-filled people in our churches praying for the grace to live in virtue, and live out that message with young people. Schools will be places of grace, with children and adults learning through everyday life about redemption, justice, and divine love.

# CHAPTER 6

## TRADITIONAL DISCIPLINE VS. VIRTUE-BASED RESTORATIVE DISCIPLINE

*"He who heeds instruction is on the path to life,*
*but he who rejects reproof goes astray."*

Proverbs 10:17

WHEN OUR PATIENCE RUNS SHORT, and a student's stamina for misbehavior seems to have no end, we are headed for disaster. As mentioned in chapter 2, in traditional systems of discipline, these students may get a "check" or demerit, or have their names written on the board, or any number of other such consequences. As the behavior continues, the frazzled teacher begins to head into quite possibly the "mom or dad lecture." He or she might say such things as, "Haven't I told you already to stop that? What are you thinking?" or, "Would you quit acting like a kindergartner? If you keep doing that I'm going to send you down to the kindergarten class and you can learn how to behave — you could learn a thing or two from them!"

In some cases, students report that they are serving "punishments" in which they are not sure why they received it. In these cases, we might hear a teacher say: "Oh, you know what you did. Just sit there and think about it." But, truthfully, what they are really trying to tell us is that the consequence for their actions is irrelevant. They do not see the connection between their behavior — what they did wrong — and what they were assigned as a consequence.

Punishments in Scripture are often prescribed for particular offenses against the poor and for those who commit offenses against others. But the distinct concern of biblical justice is not to punish sinners, but to restore peace ("Shalom") by clarifying and dealing with the damage caused by wrongdoing. Punishment was a tool to help achieve this.[46] Contrary to what many think, it is not punishment that satisfies the demands of justice, but rather acts of repentance, restoration, and renewal. How many times have we rushed to assign a punishment only to regret it when we cooled down? This has been the case with parents at home as well as with educators in school settings.

Initially, when parents are introduced to VBRD™, before fully understanding the principles and practices, they assume that because there is conversation involved in restoration, we are too "soft" on kids, and that we are just "talking away" problems instead of punishing. This argument is quickly dispelled as schools see the value in bringing closure to situations so the person who has harmed can be absolved by making things as right as possible for the target of mistreatment. This is central to the ongoing peace in classrooms with VBRD™. Punishment can serve as a mechanism for helping to promote this restoration. But the lessons in our failings can be found in the process of making things right, not simply from scolding, lecturing, detentions, etc.

This does not mean we should abolish the discipline policies currently in place. Rather, we should consider discipline policies to be living documents that have a fluidity that is responsive to the circumstance and the needs of all parties involved. Being "fair" is not the same as being "equal." In VBRD™, there is accountability and responsibility beyond what might be part of disciplinary action. For instance, if there is a detention to be served, the restorative process would call for repairing any

---

46. Chris Marshall, *The Little Book of Biblical Justice: A Fresh Approach to the Bible's Teaching on Justice* (Intercourse, PA: Good Books, 2005), p. 48.

damages and restoring broken relationships. While many readers may argue, "I already do that," it is not systematic, consistent, and scripted so that everyone administers justice in the same way. The prescriptive model presented in VBRD™ enables all adults — those at home and those at school — to bring clarity, consistency, and constancy in cultivating virtue and providing a foundation of love and forgiveness as children learn about mercy and justice.

> Compassionate acceptance of human fallibility is essential to the functioning of healthy relationships. Where failure occurs, justice must be seasoned with mercy, or it is not true justice.[47]

The Old Testament identifies such things as compensation (see Ex 21:2-36). Some demanded double restitution, or more in some cases. In the *Book of Leviticus*, if there were remorse, a thief would need to return the portion plus an extra measure (see 6:5), and an even greater portion if there was no regret, or what was stolen could not be recovered. There may be people in your community interested in exploring these ideas throughout Scripture and applying them appropriately in policies. But for this work, Jesus is the merciful Redeemer who has already paid the price, and we can respond to his call to justice in social discrimination. This is done through fellowship with sinners and outcasts as referenced in the Gospels of Matthew, Mark, and Luke.[48]

Henri Nouwen states in his book *Making All Things New*[49]: "Our lives are like overpacked suitcases. They are full, yet unfulfilled. We become restless, wondering what the purpose of the busyness is — then we become bored. Boredom comes not from a lack of anything to do, but rather the lack of meaning our day-to-day movements have in serving a higher purpose." The result is a moodiness, irritability, and frustra-

---

47. Chris Marshall, *The Little Book of Biblical Justice: A Fresh Approach to the Bible's Teaching on Justice* (Intercourse, PA: Good Books, 2005), p. 37.

48. *Ibid.*, p. 53.

49. Henri J. M. Nouwen, *Making All Things New: An Invitation to the Spiritual Life* (New York: Harper One, 1981).

tion that ekes out into our conversations and colors our relationships unfavorably.

If we were to consider a new way of seeing things in light of this understanding, perhaps our interactions would be more meaningful. The restorative model first values relationships.

> Whoever would be great among you must be your servant.' The exercise of authority is measured morally in terms of its divine origin, its reasonable nature and its specific object. No one can command or establish what is contrary to the dignity of persons and the natural law. (*CCC* 2235)

In understanding the importance of this passage, the powerful message comes in measuring our actions regarding the dignity of persons. How many times do we fail to act with dignity during a rant? How many times do we diminish a child's dignity in the process? The hurried pace of life, which can cause moodiness and irritability, may cause impatient outbursts. This dynamic spills into schools, setting us up for failure as soon as the bell rings. The best way to change this is to temper our thoughts, words, and actions, and to challenge ourselves to shape our inner dialogue with optimism. Here is the secret to meeting this challenge:

## Commit to Being constructive

If this sounds like a simple concept, try it for twenty-four hours. You will struggle—guaranteed! If you are to commit to being constructive, here's what you will need to consider:

Putting an end to:

- Gossip.

- Negative humor.

- Sarcasm.

- Negative talk toward, about, or with another person (this is different from gossip).

- Negative actions toward a person (no withholding love in any way from those with whom you are unhappy — this means a spouse, friends, children, even those relatives in whom it is a struggle to find goodness!).

Try these suggestions as an alternative to the negative list above:

- Speak kindly of others, and commit to stopping gossip with simple statements such as: "Are you sure about that?" or "Let's change the subject."

- Encourage others.

- Use humor appropriately, being careful to laugh at circumstances rather than people.

- Pay genuine compliments — intentionally and daily. (Commit to giving five a day — and pray for the opportunity to see them. God never lets us down on this one!)

- Consider the need others have for your generosity. This may be in your time, your support, your encouragement, your help with a project, or your quiet intercession in prayer. This type of generosity expresses the virtue of charity.

So this is your challenge as you read this chapter. If we are to integrate this restorative philosophy into our hallways at school, we must begin with a commitment to being constructive in relationships. This restorative model is congruent with our faith teaching. It is scriptural that we act this way — it is part of the unspoken "professional code of ethics" adults are to model. Here is the instruction we receive from Scripture:

> Let no evil talk come out of your mouths, but only such as is good for edifying, as fits the occasion, that it may impart grace to those who hear. And do not grieve the Holy Spirit of

God, in whom you were sealed for the day of redemption. Let all bitterness and wrath and anger and clamor and slander be put away from you, with all malice, and be kind to one another, tenderhearted, forgiving one another, as God in Christ forgave you. (*Ephesians* 4:29-32)

We are also encouraged to honor this commitment in *Philippians*:

Finally, brethren, whatever is true, whatever is honorable, whatever is just, whatever is pure, whatever is lovely, whatever is gracious, if there is any excellence, if there is anything worthy of praise, think about these things. (4:8)

The introduction of the "virtue base" to this model now holds us responsible for looking to God as the author and defender of our faith. When we seek God, we are asking the supernatural forces to be at work within us in the natural world. Because all virtue is good and creates goodness, we can more easily commit to being constructive, because our conversations will take on a new, more positive tone.

One teacher shared that the phrase "commit to being constructive" brought to mind "constructive criticism." Her 14-year-old daughter had been in tears over the fact that the honest remarks about her clothing hurt her feelings. "I'm just giving you constructive criticism" was the response. Be mindful that constructive means to "build up" and criticism typically means "faultfinding and judging."

Here are a few examples of the difference when using constructive communication:

**Destructive:** "I don't like the way that looks."
**Constructive:** "I like the outfit you had on the other day better than this one."

**Destructive:** "You always misbehave. I'm tired of asking you to stop."
**Constructive:** "It is hard for me to teach when you disrupt. We need a better plan. Do you have any suggestions?"

**Destructive:**     "That one family is the problem. If they would show up at the parent meetings, maybe they'd learn to be better parents or realize this isn't the right school for them."

**Constructive:**    "That family didn't make it to the parent meeting. Maybe I'll pick up an extra set of handouts and give them a call. I don't know what kept them from attending, so I can let them know what was discussed."

Your "homework" on this is to make a list of all the negative (or destructive) words or phrases you typically hear spoken either by you or those around you. Then reframe them into constructive language and begin to integrate them. Constructive communication can be honest, but it is never riddled with sarcasm or negative humor. It always maintains the dignity of the person.

We can integrate prayerful discernment of the virtue we wish to cultivate first within ourselves, then within the parties we interact with in all circumstances. This is the most difficult aspect to assimilate because it requires us to be introspective and do the soul-searching work of bettering ourselves. Many times we can easily see how others need to change or improve, yet fail to see the need within ourselves. We must be the change agents as well when seeking solutions to the difficult circumstances and relationships we encounter.

Blame and the need to be "right" may be among the top causes of failed relationships. In thinking about this idea, call to mind the arguments, the fights, and the alienation caused by these behaviors. In a marriage, it may begin with someone failing to pick up dirty socks or leaving dirty dishes in the sink for days or weeks on end. In a classroom, it begins with small tensions between two students or an adult and a student. We evaluate the situation in our minds and quickly judge the situation in our favor. We begin to divide responsibilities in our minds and decide what we will and will not do to improve the current state of the relationship. We begin drawing lines in the sand, and before long we become stuck in a rigid belief about the role we will play, seeing the other person as the problem. We also plead our case with others so as to gain support for our point of view and gain comfort in knowing we are not alone.

This is why the commitment to being constructive must prevail! Others who experience the same problems band together and may fail to reach a constructive solution. This can result in blaming poor parenting, or deciding that we know what is best and that no other plan of action can be as good as the one we have crafted. Then students may feel marginalized by adults and by peers, and we may fail to recognize this suffering with compassion.

## Comparison of Discipline Models

Many times, I have worked with schools over a period of years, teaching restorative practices. This commitment to being constructive is one of the hardest things to master. Yet, in those schools where I spend more time, this idea bears the most fruit. Restorative practices involve a firm foundation of trust, which is cultivated over time through day-to-day interactions that strengthen healthy relationships. One example of this is talking circles. In our Catholic schools, this process integrates prayer, and in VBRD™, virtue education is added. Having prayer circles for both adults at home and at school is the best way to build knowledge and trust regarding virtue and restorative discipline. As adults learn to honor relationships in this way, then children benefit from their commitment of time to experience these practices. Children are the last to learn these practices. Adults must be first to see the benefit of healthy interactions, building trust with one another, and learning about restorative practices before they can authentically teach children.

Once a teacher told me she thought she would never be able to learn these concepts. Then one day she was on the playground helping two students work out a problem when she realized she had actually learned every step of the model, and that it worked out just the way she had acquired it: "It has changed the way I think about teaching and discipline."

| Response to Typical Behaviors | Traditional Discipline | Restorative Discipline | VBRD™ |
|---|---|---|---|
| See misbehavior (bullying or other similar concern) and assign punishment. | X | | |
| Assign a punishment for the entire class based on misbehavior of a few. | X | | |
| Use unkind words when frustrated with class behaviors.. | X | | |
| Name bullying and other inappropriate behaviors as possible "harm." | | X | X |
| Understand the harm and develop empathy for both the target and the harmer. | | X | X |
| Listen/respond to the needs of person harmed and the person who harmed. | | X | X |
| Ask what rules/laws have been broken? | X | | |
| Ask who is to blame? | X | | |
| Ask what do they deserve? | X | | |
| Look at the process for carrying out school discipline. | | X | X |
| Look at how those involved are reintegrated into the classroom. | | X | X |
| Ask who has been mistreated? | | X | X. |

*(continued on next page)*

| Response to Typical Behaviors | Traditional Discipline | Restorative Discipline | VBRD™ |
|---|---|---|---|
| Ask what was the harm (i.e., physical, emotional, social, etc.)? | | X | X |
| Ask what needs to be done to repair the harm? | | X | X |
| Ask who needs to do it? | | X | X |
| Ask what agreements need to be made? | | X | X |
| Encourage responsibility and accountability through personal reflection and through a collaborative process. | | X | X |
| Create caring climates to support healthy communities | | X | X |
| Change the system when it contributes to the harm. | | X | X |
| Integrate faith as a foundation to understanding the role of virtue in preventing harm. | | | X |
| Integrate prayer/discernment of virtue education in addressing harm. | | | X |
| Integrate sacraments as often as possible to grow in grace. | | | X |

This table serves to provide further clarification regarding the added dimension of Virtue-Based Restorative Discipline™ model.

| Key Goals of Restorative Discipline with Adaptation of Virtue-Based Restorative Discipline | |
| --- | --- |
| Restorative Discipline Seeks: | Virtue-Based Restorative Discipline Seeks: |
| To understand the harm and to develop empathy for both the harmed and the harmer. | To lay a foundation of spirituality within the adult community (both at home and at school) that develops for a minimum of six weeks before working with students using the materials provided. |
| To listen and respond to the needs of the person harmed and person who harmed. | Prayerful discernment of key virtues that adults will individually begin to cultivate while collectively praying/reflecting on them. |
| To encourage responsibility and accountability through personal reflection and through a collaborative process. | To educate students on virtue through interactive class meetings. |
| To reintegrate the harmer and, if necessary, the harmed back into the school community as valuable, contributing members. | To teach students to prayerfully discern virtues they wish to cultivate and integrate the results into the process of addressing harm. |
| To create caring climates to support healthy communities. | To identify the strengthening of one's relationship with God as primary in repairing harm to relationships with others. |
| To change the system when it contributes to harm. | To create high accountability and high responsibility for solving conflicts — both for adults and students — in such a way that the cycle of harm will end. Sacramental practices will increase as they are integral to the process. |

When acting out of virtue, reflect first on yours by asking such questions as:

- What virtue am I operating from?

- Could others see the virtue in me?

- Have I genuinely complimented someone today?

- Did the compliment mention a virtue?

- How can I do better tomorrow?

This chapter is an important foundation for understanding your style of communication as it relates to discipline. Many adults working with VBRD™ have discovered the missing link in their success: They are operating out of traditional patterns of discipline. The "my way or the highway" mentality cannot coexist with this new model. Traditional discipline is based in faultfinding, and restoration is based in constantly evaluating for improvement.

You are using a traditional model if you find yourself using H.U.R.T.:

H. Having trouble seeing anyone's perspective other than your own.
U. Unwilling to pray or share your virtue.
R. Regretting the way you handled the situation afterward.
T. Talking too much, asking too little.

You are on the right track if you find yourself using H.E.L.P.:

H. Having involved parties do most of the talking.
E. Everyone seeking solutions rather than blaming.
L. Listening with compassion.
P. Praying and speaking about virtue, integrating sacraments.

In committing to the restorative model, consider what you desire in your relationships. Do you want harmony? It takes self-confidence to reach out to those relationships we find challenging. Stepping outside our circle of friends to make new acquaintances, or choosing to help children overcome obstacles to making friends with their peers is a worthwhile endeavor.

By being open to listening more, and talking less, you will help those around you feel valued. Upholding the dignity of the human person is the expectation God sets for us. Our foundation of virtue serves as the moral compass by which we live, and we can challenge others to do the same. Virtue always serves the greater good. Virtue reinforces the commitment to being constructive, and it also plays a vital role in the restorative model. Holding relationships as the most important priority is the common theme within our faith teaching and within this model.

# CHAPTER 7

## A FRAMEWORK FOR
## A NEW VISION

*"And he who sat upon the throne said, 'Behold, I make all things new.'*
*Also he said, 'Write this, for these words are trustworthy and true.'"*

Revelations 21:5

PERHAPS YOU HAVE SERVED on committees over the years that have passed recommendations for changes in policy or procedure for an organization or institution. Change can be met with resistance because there are risks involved. Consequences may be difficult to calculate in advance. When virtue is at work, it not only makes change easier, but it also provides a guarantee of success in Catholic schools, parishes, and homes because it works for the good. VBRD™ helps to create systematic change in the way adults approach interactions in which children are mistreated.

In most bullying prevention programs, the primary outcome is to decrease bullying behaviors. In VBRD™, however, there are two expected outcomes:

### Decrease antisocial behavior

- Bullying behaviors — These are ongoing, escalating hurtful words/ actions intended to harm, humiliate, or intimidate a target having

97

a difficult time defending himself or herself. (See chapter 2 for a complete definition.)

- Disruptive behaviors — This is any behavior that takes time away from teaching and learning but is not necessarily directed toward another student — for instance, making noises or throwing paper during class.

## Increase faith practices

- Evangelization — This is part of our faith teaching, and to integrate it into the way we interact around harm provides an opportunity to share our faith in a meaningful, practical way.

- Virtue education — Becoming a "student of virtue" can allow us to learn to operate in the natural world while we are mindful of our higher calling to live a life of moral integrity. God wants us to grow in our love for him and for one another. Virtue invites us to that deeper experience in our daily lives.

- Practices — Virtue draws us closer to God, giving us the desire for intimacy through sacramental grace. This means having a desire for attendance at Mass, the Sacrament of Reconciliation, Adoration of the Blessed Sacrament, etc.

The Logic Model on the next page illustrates the outline regarding goals.

## DETERMINING READINESS FOR VBRD™

You may be a current VBRD™ school or parish community member reading this book for the first time, and finding information useful for the current efforts at home or at school. In either case, this section will be helpful in assessing where you and your community are in your understanding and implementation readiness. Many schools are "gung-ho" as they begin, soon to realize it is difficult to get everyone to implement with

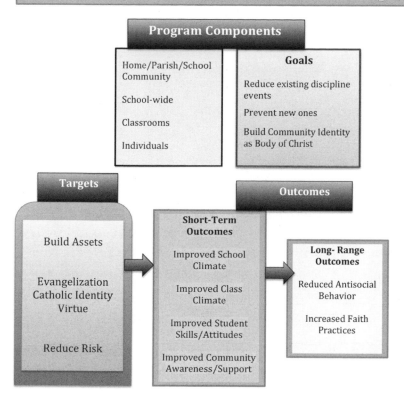

Logic Model For Virtue-Based Restorative Discipline ™

fidelity. Some schools start out strong, but perhaps the key team member becomes ill, or becomes too busy to coordinate the team-implementation plan. Some of our most successful teams started slowly, working through confusion and uncertainty. Then one day VBRD™ became the catalyst for success and new enthusiasm when using the step-by-step process to miraculously (literally!) resolve a serious incident. These teams become star performers because they know it can work.

Many factors can affect good implementation, and your work can only be as successful as the least willing team members, staff, or parents. Those having constant contact with children are significant change agents, so teachers and parents are key players. However, administrators must be 100 percent supportive to the process and to ongoing train-

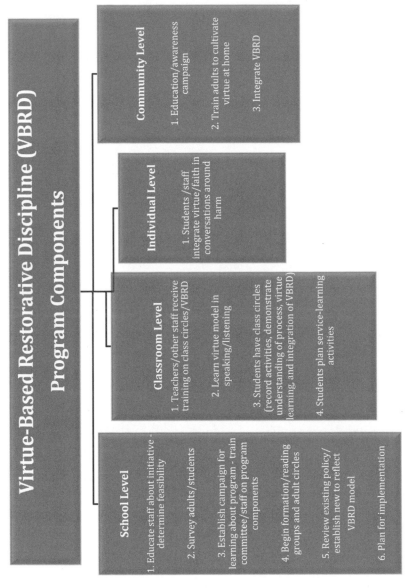

## Virtue-Based Restorative Discipline (VBRD) Program Components

**School Level**

1. Educate staff about initiative - determine feasibility

2. Survey adults/students

3. Establish campaign for learning about program - train committee/staff on program components

4. Begin formation/reading groups and adult circles

5. Review existing policy/ establish new to reflect VBRD model

6. Plan for implementation

**Classroom Level**

1. Teachers/other staff receive training on class circles/VBRD

2. Learn virtue model in speaking/listening

3. Students have class circles (record activities, demonstrate understanding of process, virtue learning, and integration of VBRD)

4. Students plan service-learning activities

**Individual Level**

1. Students /staff integrate virtue/faith in conversations around harm

**Community Level**

1. Education/awareness campaign

2. Train adults to cultivate virtue at home

3. Integrate VBRD

Celebrate Year End and Plan for Year Two

ing in order to support the efforts of all adults. A self-assessment can be helpful in considering whether or not VBRD™ is possible in your home, school, or parish community (visit www.virtuebase.org). The self-assessment provided can be given to those you have gathered to prayerfully discern if this is an effort you are ready to begin, If you can check off most of these questions, then you are ready to proceed with discussions about next steps. VBRD™ is a comprehensive, schoolwide initiative that must be an integral part of the community so everyone experiences the benefit. The evidence base for VBRD™ rests in the surveys, which are available as part of the process. Assuring fidelity to the model and getting the technical support necessary for successful implementation will help your team, staff, parents, and broader community gain confidence in their ability to achieve the desired outcomes. This can lead to a certification process, which is granted after meeting required criteria. More information is available though the Web site www.virtuebase.org.

This model requires a minimum of five adults to successfully implement and monitor progress. The administration must be the first to commit. Then, two staff members should be selected who exhibit optimism, peer support, and organizational ability. These individuals will coordinate the activities for reflection and help with training staff to facilitate class meetings with the format provided for teaching virtues. Two parents will also be essential as the cheerleaders for their peer group and coordinators for meetings and learning and reflection sessions on virtue for parents. These committee members must be committed to the spiritual enrichment provided for virtue education, the foundation for adults.

After completing the checklist for determining readiness, your school community can begin preparation by ordering necessary training materials at www.virtuebase.org.

## TIMELINE FOR IMPLEMENTATION

### Month One

STAFF

- Receive overview, decide to implement.

- Form VBRD™ Team.

- Decide what virtues the school will work on: one key virtue for the year, and an additional virtue each quarter.

- Determine the campaign name — it must include virtue in the slogan.

- Complete survey.

- Read this book chapter by chapter.

- Set a date for a parent meeting within the next two months.

- Begin the personal reflection process on virtue formation for six sessions — resources provided in appendix 3.

### Months Two-Four

PARENTS

- Receive overview.

- Complete survey.

- Set calendar dates for further readings.

- Receive materials for reflection — resources provided.

STUDENTS

- Complete survey.

STAFF

- Continue reflections/discussions.

- Complete in-service on Living Your Mission.

- Review/revise discipline policy.

- Train teachers to facilitate class meetings.

- Discuss ways to teach virtues/set virtues for the year.

- Identify resources for teaching virtues.

- Set up procedures for discipline in restorative-virtue model.

## Months 5+

- Class meetings, parent meetings, staff meetings all reflect virtue model.

- Full implementation of new model, survey again at 12 months.

The program components should reach every level of the school community. In order for your efforts to succeed, there must be a shared responsibility and a shared accountability for all. No one person can "save the school." While you may have some very effective leaders, they cannot shoulder the responsibility for keeping discipline manageable. When everyone works together to effect change, the result is much more powerful. The next chapter will detail specific aspects of this time-line for implementation.

# CHAPTER 8

## STEPS TO
## IMPLEMENTATION

*"For the commandment is a lamp and the teaching a light,
and the reproofs of discipline are the way of life."*

Proverbs 6:23

DISCIPLINE MUST HAVE SHORT- AND LONG-TERM GOALS, recognizing the end result as a process that leads children to become responsible adults. This chapter will help readers see the continuum of implementation in order to prepare for long-term goals. Here are the first steps:

- Gather a few people together and pray about it. "For where two or three are gathered in my name, there am I in the midst of them" (Mt 18:20). Make a list of what you are looking for in a discipline program for your school.

- Pick a date to give an overview — materials are available in the appendix and at www.virtuebase.org, such as "Principles to Live By."

- Pull your school community together and educate at every level about what you want to accomplish.

| Timeline for Implementation of Virtue-Based Restorative Discipline | | | | | |
| --- | --- | --- | --- | --- | --- |
| MONTHS | 1 | 2 | 3 | 4 | 5 |
| Form Team | X | | | | |
| Get Overview | X | | | | |
| Survey Staff, Students, Parents | | X | | | |
| Begin Staff Reflections | | X | | | |
| Begin Parent Reflections | | | X | | |
| Team and Staff Training | | | X | X | X |
| Work on Mission | | | | X | |
| Work on Discipline Policy | | | | | X |
| 1. Pick School Virtues 2. Name Campaign 3. Commissioning Mass | | | | | |
| Begin Class Meetings | | | | | |
| Implement Full Program | | | | | |
| Monitor Progress | | | | X | X |
| Survey Again | | | | | |
| Ongoing Training | | | | | |
| Compare Results with Baseline | | | | | |
| Use Other Resources for Reflection/Training | | | | | |

| 6 | 7 | 8 | 9 | 10 | 11 | 12 | 13 |
|---|---|---|---|----|----|----|----|
|   |   |   |   |    |    |    |    |
|   |   |   |   |    |    |    |    |
|   |   |   |   |    |    |    |    |
| X | X | X | X |    |    |    |    |
|   |   |   |   |    |    |    |    |
| X |   |   |   |    |    |    |    |
|   | X |   |   |    |    |    |    |
|   |   | X |   |    |    |    |    |
| X | X | X | X | X  |    |    |    |
|   |   |   |   |    |    | X  |    |
|   |   |   |   | X  | X  | X  | X  |
|   |   |   |   |    |    |    | X  |
|   | X | X | X | X  | X  | X  | X  |

- Using the timeline, track your progress (see timeline on pages 106–107). Make sure your committees are on board with your efforts.

Virtue is the foundation from which implementation begins. This involves a comprehensive, cross-curricular modeling of virtue both at home and at school.

Restorative discipline is a process to involve, as fully as possible, those who have a stake in a specific offense. Those people identify and address the harms, needs, and obligations of those involved in order to heal and put things as right as possible.

First and foremost, the role of all team members is to pray for the success of these efforts. The peace that passes all human understanding cannot exist without it. The team members will encourage others along the way and work to model the kindness we want to see in students.

## Role of Administrator

- Commit to personal development of virtues.

- Support the overall initiative.

- Inform school board and parish council.

- Help staff understand the process and support the necessary changes in policy and procedure. This is a unique way of seeing behavior and requires a new vision.

- Approve the calendar for various activities.

- Be open to and familiar with new ways to respond to harm — this is critical.

## Role of Staff on Team

- Commit to personal development of virtues.

- Coordinate various times/places for staff reflection circles (weekly or biweekly).

- Coordinate bulletin boards for monthly virtue activities.

- Help staff with class-meeting themes, support facilitation of meetings.

- Help with surveying students and staff.

- Be optimistic about the effort; commit to being constructive.

## Role of Parents on Team

- Commit to personal development of virtues.

- Coordinate information sessions for parents.

- Coordinate survey for parents; assist with students if possible.

- Coordinate parent reflection circles once weekly or biweekly if possible.

- Coordinate take-home materials on virtues for parent education.

- Support the efforts of the school — be there in person, or speak positively when attending school/parish events; commit to being constructive.

The team will benefit from co-leadership, that includes one school staff person and one parent. The co-leaders share the responsibility for overseeing the efforts, leading meetings, and conducting follow-up activities. Most importantly, they should stay connected to their VBRD™ training contact to maintain certification. There are compliance checkpoints along the way that must be fulfilled in order to assure ongoing positive outcomes. VBRD™ trainers can provide technical support when needed, as well as ongoing resources to further the work you have begun in your school. Annual surveys will give evidence that your work is successful and provide guidance in areas of need. See chapter 13 for more details.

# CHAPTER 9

## BEGINNING WITH ADULTS AT SCHOOL

*"Tend the flock of God that is your charge, not by constraint but willingly, not for shameful gain but eagerly, not as domineering over those in your charge but being examples to the flock. And when the chief Shepherd is manifested you will obtain the unfading crown of glory."*

1 Peter 5:2-4

AS MENTIONED EARLIER IN CHAPTER 2, OBPP is a recognized program created by Dr. Dan Olweus. He states clearly that it is up to adults to reduce and prevent the problem of school bullying. Some may disagree, arguing that students should be responsible for their behavior, and the OBPP agrees with this belief. But, adults must first create a safe environment, ensuring that students can report problems and enlist the help of adults in stopping peer abuse. Adults hold class meetings, provide procedures for reporting and engage adults at home in responding to behaviors.

The OBPP directive to train adults first is a great model for implementing any prevention program. In my many years of bullying prevention work, both as a developer of curriculum for students and as a certified Olweus Trainer, I've found that simply working with students will not stop bullying. Unless adults create a seamless systematic change with consistent language and responsiveness to bullying, students will not be confident in finding their school environment safe from harm. Many times, teachers fail to recognize nonverbal cues or the areas of the school without adult supervision that become places of pain for children. In addition, when adults fail to treat all students with God-given dignity, both the harmer and the harmed, then the system fails students.

In traditional discipline systems, there is a need to blame someone for the offense, and someone will be punished. In VBRD™, however, we look for the acts of virtue we can celebrate — beginning with adults who have been prayerfully discerning how they can love and inspire young people by modeling a better way of being. But this process MUST begin with adults, and here are the steps:

- Surveying adults and students so that you can measure projected outcomes.

- Talking to the teachers and staff in your school community. Then, committing to studying and implementing restorative practices, such as teacher reflection circles, that will help you model care, respect, and sensitivity.

- Practicing what a peace-filled, caring classroom looks like and taking a look at the routines, procedures, and practices in every classroom.

- Building a new discipline structure that is restorative in nature and learning methods to teach conflict resolution at every level.

- Teaching parents these techniques.

- Talking in every classroom about virtues.

- Producing a written *Virtue-Based Restorative Discipline Policy* within six months of beginning the process, although it will continue to be a work in progress as your school adapts to this new model.

In working with school personnel, use the "Adult Sessions for Virtue Formation" worksheets in appendix 3 to kickstart adult talking circles. These formative first steps should take place weekly after the initial survey and continue for six consecutive weeks. A spiritual book study can keep the message alive after this initial formation. This is a basic model of catechizing adults using virtue as the foundation. After the foundational reflection circles for adults, your staff may continue meeting (no less than twice monthly) to discuss individual chapters of two popular books we have used:

- *The Hidden Power of Kindness*, by Lawrence Lovasik[50]

- *The Virtue Driven Life*, by Father Benedict J. Groeshel, C.F.R.[51]

Discussion questions are available for circle discussions in each chapter. In setting up your staff formation process, these guidelines are recommended for optimum benefit:

- Staff should have several choices of times/places for reflection circles to accommodate individual needs and schedules. Most staff coordinators will have a sign-up schedule for various times — before or after school, or during common breaks such as lunch. Staff can change groups/times from one session to the next according to their needs.

- These gatherings must be a time for personal reflection, free of discussion about school-related issues such as schedules, student problems, academics, etc.

- Hold the meeting time to no longer than 30 minutes — preferably 20 minutes. Staying on topic and honoring everyone's time is critical.

---

50. Lawrence G. Lovasik, *The Hidden Power of Kindness: A Practical Handbook for Souls Who Dare to Transform the World, One Deed at a Time* (Manchester, NH: Sophia Institute Press, 1999).

51. Father Benedict Groeschel, *The Virtue Driven Life* (Huntington, IN: Our Sunday Visitor, 2006).

- There may be some times when the discussions are longer, but this should be noted in advance.

- Every voice counts — so each person in the group should have equal time to speak. No one person should dominate.

- If your staff has professional learning communities, these can be tied in so there is not extra effort — just begin with a brief circle discussion prior to the other work of the groups.

These guidelines will be clear as your staff begins to schedule/implement these reflection circles. Learning this process is important for all staff (non-teaching staff included), particularly as they begin facilitating class meetings. The reverence of this circle process upholds the dignity of each person and will be integral to the success of the overall effort because the format provides a unique venue for speaking and listening. The feedback from this process is continually positive. Participants report feeling respected by peers and that their comments hold a particular value that transcends criticism and judgment, leading to clarity and purposeful discussion. This is valuable in establishing deeper, more meaningful relationships within families, classrooms, and beyond.

## Steps to Schoolwide Implementation of Virtue-Based Restorative Discipline™

Staff coordinators, with the input of all staff, can discern which virtues (and how many) to work on in a given year. These virtues will be:

- integrated into a campaign name — for example, Called to Kindness, Invested in Virtue, etc.

- taught to students.

- integrated into the curriculum as much as possible.

- used in conversation as much as possible.

- easily associated with behaviors, saints, and fruits of the virtue.

- identified by others observing the words and actions of staff and students.

- integrated into genuine compliments as part of the commitment to being constructive.

- featured in bulletin-board elements.

- featured in pictures of students living out the virtues.

- featured in cartoon strips about virtue by students.

- highlighted in essays, stories, fables, poems, songs.

- profiled in historical figures.

- expanded upon in seasonal-themed projects — for example, students can write letters about people they are thankful for and why those people are important, and the letters can be placed on a wall dedicated to being thankful for the bounty of kindness.

The entire school will be involved in one virtue every four to six weeks, depending on how the school decides to structure its virtue education. Teachers can create reflection circles for themselves on each virtue if this is helpful to expand understanding. Because this is new within the context of school discipline, there is very little information on virtues available to integrate into this schoolwide process. Incentive programs for the entire school for each virtue can rely on the creativity of staff. Be sure to record your tools and incentives for future reference. The capacity to expand this process into meaningful expressions of what it means to be alive in Christ is limitless.

## Naming the Campaign

If you want people to know and remember what you are doing, give them a phrase that summarizes the "mission" of your efforts. Consider how you might begin to promote your efforts in the school community.

Here are some examples of campaign names adopted by schools:

Called to Kindness

Conquer with Kindness

Kindness Takes Courage

It's a Matter of Virtues

Value Virtue

Growing in Grace

Virtue Matters

This simple step, naming, helps to galvanize thinking around what your school community is doing to address bullying. You will also need a tag line that says something about VBRD™, so that the community will understand you are addressing bullying behavior through this work and not simply "being kind." This will be important when parents seeking to enroll their children in your school ask what you are doing to address bullying behavior. Your tag line might look something like this:

Called to Kindness (large print on front of a sign or T-shirt)
We're into VBRD™ (small tag line on front, or with sponsors on back of shirt)

Conquer with Kindness
A Virtue-Based Restorative Discipline School

This simple step of naming your campaign will generate support for and enthusiasm about your efforts. It also will generate curiosity and offer opportunities to talk about what you are doing. Your VBRD™ Team will be able to translate each area of implementation into specific tasks that will show measurable outcomes. You can add this information to your discipline policy handbook.

# CHAPTER 10

# BRINGING PARENTS ON BOARD

*"Besides this, we have had earthly fathers to discipline us and we respected them. Shall we not much more be subject to the Father of spirits and live? For they disciplined us for a short time at their pleasure, but he disciplines us for our good, that we may share his holiness."*

Hebrews 12:9-10

VIRTUE EDUCATION IS THE ANSWER to the many failed bullying prevention programs. Using the word "harm" or "mistreatment" in the restorative discipline model replaces the confusion caused by the vague term of "bullying," which seems to be a catchall for many behaviors that are not necessarily bullying. By referring to the definition in chapter 2, we are reminded that bullying must include: the intent to harm, escalating and repeated patterns, and the imbalance of power. Many times in an isolated incident, a student is quickly labeled a "bully." Sadly, the stickiness of labels (name-calling is a form of verbal bullying!) leaves a student stuck with an injustice that can seem irreversible. Parents can greatly benefit by shifting from the problem-focus of bullying to the solution-focus of virtue-building.

It seems that in nearly every school implementing a comprehensive program to address bullying, parents applaud the school's efforts to address this painful behavior and express relief that the school is so valiantly attempting to end this social injustice. They are supportive when the revised handbook for the new school year includes a great-looking policy that states there is no tolerance for cruel behavior, and it seems everyone is off to a good start.

Then sometime around October, the first bullying incident occurs. The staff is armed with the right intervention and the right consequence and hauls kids off to the office. The students have a chat with the principal, who phones the parents. Suddenly, that brilliant program becomes a bit tarnished as parents rush to defend their child. After all, that *other* student has been the one doing the bullying, not *my* child. It's about time so-and-so got a dose of his own medicine! Thus begins the downward spiral of the bullying program. Now the teacher and/or principal is "bullying my child," giving demerits or checkmarks or whatever that new policy calls for. "But it's not fair!" parents say in the parking lot, on the phone, over dinner, on Facebook, in texts and tweets.

So many times parents hear only half of the story. It is typically the half about the other child involved, not what their child has done to provoke a situation. We instinctively want to protect our children — this is the way God created us. So it seems counterintuitive to support the administration in its effort to keep a peaceful school if it means our child is at fault and must be corrected.

How can we avoid this scenario? It is my deeply held belief that if Catholic schools are to keep their doors open for the next generation, we must all work to evangelize everyone within our school communities, most especially parents. Each of us must prayerfully discern what this means for us both individually and collectively. Virtue education can be a solution to parents' challenge to remain objective, as well as a way to help them see social injustice with greater perspective. Our faith teaches us to consider the greater good, yet we struggle when our personal interests, particularly our children, are at stake.

We must expect from parents the same high responsibility and high accountability that we are asking of our students and staff. So many times parents say they wish they could do a better job of setting limits and disciplining their children. With this in mind, we can give parents some simple supportive materials to initiate virtue education at home with their children and in small groups with other parents.

When a child comes home and reports a painful encounter with others, here are some key questions parents can ask:

- Did you tell an adult?

- What did the adults do when this happened?

- If this person were here to tell the other side of the story, what would we hear?

- Can you think of a way this could have been avoided?

- If you had a do-over, would you have done anything differently? What do you think might have happened if you did?

- What do you think needs to happen next to make things right?

- Why do you think this happened?

The best response is always a great question! Questions illuminate truth if asked out of genuine curiosity and love. Children can develop critical-thinking skills. When they fail, we can help them find new solutions by asking them questions that cause them to think creatively about their circumstances. If we help them think through the harm they have caused, they will own the behavior. Then, they will own the responsibility to make things right again. We will no longer need the "lecture" that tells them what they did, how they disappointed us, and how they will be fittingly punished.

When problems arise at school, children need to be encouraged to seek adult help in solving problems. They should do this immediately, rather than waiting to tell an adult at home, where the issue might be taken out of context. Students can identify adults they might seek out when help is needed. Many times, a child's perception of an experience can become distorted between the time it occurs and the time the child gets home. Schools repeatedly report that disgruntled parents show up to complain about an ongoing problem their child is facing only to discover that principals and teachers are hearing about it for the first time.

What causes this? Perhaps children want to simply vent their frustration without expecting adult action, but soon realize their parents will overreact. They may eventually choose to withhold information to avoid the fallout. Many parents report, "I listen to my child's stories about the mean things that happen at school, but my son/daughter tells me I can't talk about it with his/her teacher." Perhaps, when the teacher finally hears from the parent, he or she may have already addressed the situation. In these cases, virtue can help immeasurably.

One final thought regarding incidents at school: Staff must be instructed to contact parents before the end of the school day. This will only take a few minutes, but can save countless hours spent correcting a misunderstanding. If a student causes harm, the parent needs to be notified — preferably with the student present. If a student has been harmed, the parent needs to be notified of how the student's needs have been addressed. This can be very reassuring to both student and parent. It can also provide vital information about restoring equity. This builds trust. If other students witness harm and have been responsive in a helpful way, their parents should also be contacted to acknowledge the good, virtuous actions of their child. If parents can expect the school to contact them when incidents occur, then parents should expect their children to talk to adults when necessary. That's much better than waiting until school is over, when nothing can be done to immediately establish justice.

## THE CHRISTIAN FAMILY

The Christian family constitutes a specific revelation and realization of ecclesial communion, and . . . [is] called a domestic church. It is a community of faith, hope, and charity; it assumes singular importance in the Church, as is evident in the New Testament.

The Christian family is a communion of persons, a sign and image of the communion of the Father and the Son in the Holy Spirit. In the procreation and education of children it reflects the Father's work of creation. It is called to partake of the prayer and sacrifice of Christ. Daily prayer and the reading of the Word of God strengthen it in charity. The Christian family has an evangelizing and missionary task.

The relationships within the family bring an affinity of feelings, affections and interests, arising above all from the members' respect for one another. The family is a privileged community called to achieve a "sharing of thought and common deliberation by the spouses as well as their eager cooperation as parents in the children's upbringing." (*CCC* 2204-2206)

This statement gives us inspiration and motivation to evangelize our children, because we have the privilege of being their first witnesses of faith. It can be a simple Sign of the Cross on their forehead as we pray over them. We can sing about Jesus. We can teach them their first prayers, and we can take them to Mass. Living by example the teachings of Christ is one of the most gratifying acts of faith we can offer our children. It is not enough to simply teach our children. It is more important that we truly internalize our own response to God. We must be tireless in living a sacramental and virtuous life first for ourselves, then for others. That is the beauty of God's command, that we love others as we love ourselves after first coming to know, love and serve him.

This means we should learn the holy habits that can lead us to our heavenly home, and these virtuous habits will draw us so close to God that we cannot imagine our lives without him. Because he is the giver of all gifts, we want to share that gift with our most precious possessions — our children. So we are not alone in our efforts toward mercy, compassion, kindness, love, and other such virtues. We have a constant companion with us who longs for our affection, and as we share Christ with our children, he shares them with us. They are a created act of his divine kindness, just as all creation is. They belong to him, and we are the stewards to show them the way to his Sacred Heart.

When parents can learn to see their children through this sacred lens, everything changes in the way harm is handled  at school. Parents can then make every undesirable behavior an opportunity to grow in virtue. So, by prayerfully discerning what virtues to personally demonstrate in times of conflict, parents can express the spirit of their intent in a constructive way. For instance, to demonstrate forgiveness as a virtue, then parents could think carefully about how this would apply to the child's circumstance at school. Your response to an incident might be: "Because I am working on the virtue of forgiveness, I'm willing to let you explain what happened and come up with a plan we can both agree to in making things right." This requires thoughtful reflection on everyone's part to creatively consider an alternative to the traditional discipline model.

As parents begin their role on the VBRD™ Team, they will be the leaven in the parent community. They can schedule multiple opportunities for other parents to be involved. Consider these options:

- Inviting parents to attend morning coffee circles after all-school Masses

- Asking parents to help with survey permission forms for students and planning for effective parent survey participation

- Asking parents to participate in six-week virtue circles with the reflections provided in appendix 3

- Encouraging parents to learn and practice circle processes with other adults and with families at home

- Challenging parents to pray more with their children

- Suggesting that parents consider as a family how they are disciplining and practicing the VBRD™ formula for addressing harm at home among siblings, in assigning chores, etc.

- Encouraging parents to journal and pray about virtue, and to committing to a constructive way of living

- Promoting efforts for the broader parish community on Sundays

- Signing up new team members at open houses or beginning reading groups

- Choosing virtue reading for Church liturgical seasons

- Volunteering to do small book studies in homes

- Helping with classroom virtue projects

- Working on banners for school hallways, the cafeteria, etc.

- Hosting discussion circles on selected topics (cyber safety, homework, summer fun, etc.) and determining how virtue can be integrated into these topics

One parent group spent time on a parent newsletter for each virtue the school was working on, sharing ideas, reading materials, information, and parent perspectives on how the virtue could help their parenting at home. They did an exceptional job. When these projects are finished, it is important to discuss how these efforts can make us better people, being perfected for heaven. But remember that it is not enough to talk about virtue — we must be dedicated to living virtue as a way of life.

The most important aspect of involving parents is to bring them to a closer encounter with Jesus Christ. When this occurs, the virtue work will change family life. Using virtue in discipline, recognizing the need to be constructive, and prayer will all bring the fruits of peace, harmony, and unity needed in our homes today.

# CHAPTER 11

## TEACHING OUR CHILDREN

*"The wolf shall dwell with the lamb, and the leopard shall lie down with the kid, and the calf and the lion and the fatling together, and a little child shall lead them."*

Isaiah 11:6

As mentioned in earlier chapters, Dr. Dan Olweus believes that adults are responsible for setting the climate for safe schools. Adults are the thermostats — they are to set the expectations in our homes and schools. Children are the thermometers — they will rise to the "temperature" of the expectations we set. How many times have we had tantrums with an audience of young witnesses? Honestly, every adult fails at times. However, with the VBRD™ model, we are called to have a more prayerful, Christ-centered journey, viewing the ups and downs of everyday life with new perspective.

After your initial surveys, adult reflection, and a review of current practices in discipline, it is time to begin introducing students to this new way of seeing harmful behavior. You will no longer use the word "bullying," and students will begin to see adults taking more time to pray and reflect. In an introductory session with one school, the staff discussed the desire to pray together in the mornings, but they felt that when students entered the building, the activity would be disrupted. One teacher said that the seventh-graders would laugh if they saw teachers gathered in the hallway praying. This challenging question was posed: What if we asked the students if we could pray without disturbance and count on their reverent respect during this time?

Expecting students to provide the time and space for prayer is not asking too much. Especially if we have morning prayer with them just minutes later as the school day begins. Policy and procedures such as daily adult prayer or morning circles can become part of the daily routine, and we can expect students to honor this, knowing that it is meant to serve their needs in a fuller way. Just as we fail at times, we also know that we can do better. It is the same with young people — we must expect great things from them because they can do better. High accountability and high responsibility mean that we will challenge them to model adult behavior; however, we must first model it for them.

There can be nothing more comforting to children than seeing the significant adults in their lives living in harmony. This has transcendent value for them and for us. It is the comfort of knowing that your parents are getting along and your teachers are happy, and all these things filter down to kinder interactions for everyone. These are the fruits of living a virtuous life. When students begin to comment on the virtue they see in us, we have won them over! This is a true sign that we are living a virtue. For this reason, it is important that adults work on their part before bringing students into the picture.

When you are ready to introduce students to VBRD™, student surveys establish the base line for data outcomes if your school is seeking certification. You must be able to measure your successes and realign to improve in areas of need. In the first year, conduct a survey at the beginning and at the end of the year. If there's any confusion among students, you can inform them that the efforts to train them will begin after the survey is completed. But giving them answers to the questions so that they understand them is, well, giving them the answers! Instead, you can simply state, "If there is a definition that you are unclear about, just do your best." You can restate the question in a different way if they do not understand it. Students in younger grades will need to have each question read aloud slowly. Be sure student answers are confidential. Teachers and survey administrators should assure students that this privacy is in place.

If you do not have all of the permission forms signed, have your VBRD™ Team parents call to obtain verbal permission, and document that prior to surveying. Make it clear that if a parent does not want a child surveyed, this will not prevent that child from participating in the ongoing work at school.

Once the surveying is complete, you can begin to hold class meetings, if your school does not already schedule them. These are essential to virtue education, the prayerful integration of virtue in daily life, and to building community within the Body of Christ in the classroom.

Class meetings for students follow the same format as the adult model. However, it is critical that teachers recognize the fragile relationships within a classroom and assure this time is sacred. So, if there is a student who is marginalized, be sure the seating is well planned so this student is not next to or across from someone who might attempt to ridicule others by inappropriate laughter, eye rolling, talking over other voices, etc.

## IMPLEMENTING CIRCLES WITH STUDENTS

- Begin by teaching them the circle process for class meetings.

- Place chairs/desks in a circle — making sure you can see each person's eyes. (This creates equality of presence.)

- Begin and end with prayer or a song.

- Select a talking piece — something that is passed as each person speaks and, as held, representing that that person is the only voice for this moment. (This creates reverence for each individual.) Students may have one "pass," in which they choose not to speak when it is their turn.

- Allow for a "one-word check-in."

- Make sure all understand the importance of honoring each person as they speak — no side comments or cross-talking.

- Give the topic for the day, and allow one or two passes for brief discussion. Try not to allow any one person to dominate the circle.

- Allow for a "one-word check-out" before ending with a prayer.

- Remind students that what is shared in the circle is not to be discussed outside that time. Let them know that if they have something personal to discuss, they should speak with you privately beforehand to determine whether or not it is appropriate to share. Or perhaps guide them in ways to appropriately express ideas or thoughts. Nothing can be more painful and compromising to the emotional safety of the circle than students discussing someone's story or emotion on the playground! (This is critical. If a child shares something personal, the teacher can say, "Let's save that for later.")

Begin with simple topics, such as favorite foods, the lunch menu, etc. This allows students to grow familiar with the purpose and structure of the talking circle. As time goes on, teachers can begin to integrate virtue sessions into the circle. If your school finds this process difficult, it is also acceptable to leave desks in their ordinary configuration and simply pass the talking piece. To optimize the sharing and openness to hearing one another, however, the circle is ideal.

Some of the discussion themes that have been extremely helpful to adults in shaping discipline policy can be brought to student circles, such as:

- What does the term restorative discipline mean to you?

- What would be different about our school if we all worked on two virtues?

- How could our discipline policy be improved to be more fair?

- What are some virtues you see in others here in your class?

Guidelines for keeping a circle can be useful for adults and students, particularly during the important formation work as a school community begins to implement VBRD™. You may simplify the language in the guidelines and assign students to read them aloud before you begin the discussion to assure you have agreement. Adults, too, can benefit from hearing these aloud as a reminder about cross-talking, giving advice, or attempting to "fix" a problem expressed by someone. Talking negatively about specific people and their comments after the circle ends can also be problematic in building trust among staff.

## Implementing Circles with Adults and Children

We've included a sheet in appendix 4 of this book listing the basic steps of a "Circle of Understanding about Virtues." Before you begin with a prayer, be sure to emphasize the goal of creating equity by reading to the group:

- In our discussion circle today, we will talk about_____, and it will take about _____ minutes.

- First we will begin with a prayer, and then we will have a one-word check-in. This is one word that describes our mood or our experience right now. It can be any word you want to say.

- The circle is a place where all of us can express ourselves without the risk of being criticized, judged, or marginalized. (For younger people: without feeling like we fit in or others will make fun of us.)

- Only one person will speak at a time, and it is the person with the talking piece. Please refrain from responding spontaneously to someone else's comments. (For younger: Please do not talk out of turn about what someone else says.)

- Be careful in your expression of nonverbals, laughter, or other sounds, as these can deeply compromise the sense of emotional safety in the circle. (For younger: If we laugh at someone else, or make a face, it may cause that person to feel unsafe, and then that person may not share again. Each of you is too important to have that happen here.)

- Each of you is given the right to "pass" once during our circle.

- As facilitator, I may ask a question to clarify or to direct others if necessary, but my role is to allow you to have the freedom to express your thoughts. Be mindful of the great dignity we each possess. (I can talk without the talking piece if I need to ask a question. I care so much about your feelings that I want to understand you, and want you to feel free to share.)

- As you take your turn, please keep your comments brief so everyone has a chance to speak. If we have time for extra discussion, do not take two turns to speak again, as this will keep someone else from having one.

- What we do and say in the circle cannot be discussed outside of this time. It would be breaking trust to talk about a person or a situation, and we expect you to honor one another in this way. If this expectation is not kept, there will be consequences. This guarantees we can depend on each other, which can allow us to talk about really important things without feeling betrayed. (Break this down so they have full understanding.)

- Can we all agree to these things? (You can do a thumbs up or down, and let everyone know that if any of these agreements are not honored, you may step in and address the situation.)

- We will begin and end with a prayer.

## Format of Weekly Class Meetings for Teaching Virtues

When each new virtue is introduced schoolwide, class meetings can follow the same simple format, and teachers can adapt for grade-level variances.

## Class Meeting One: Introduce the Virtue

- Begin the discussion by introducing the word and asking what students think it means.

- Ask someone to find the appropriate Catholic definition to share with the group.

- Ask the group, "What will it look like when we see others living this virtue?"

- Pass out a "Virtue Recognition Card" that identifies behaviors that show virtue (available at www.virtuebase.org).

- Finally, issue to students a schoolwide challenge. (To be determined in advance by your VBRD™ Team. There must be a way to recognize this virtue in the building, perhaps with incentives such as prayer cards of the saints who lived and modeled this virtue)

## Class Meeting Two: Review the Virtue and Definition

- Ask, "How many of you saw this virtue in your classmates? Please share."

- Ask, "How many of you tried to show this virtue? Please share."

- Assign two or three students to come up with examples of this virtue for the next meeting — from books of saints or other literature.

- See the "Virtue Interview Form" at www.virtuebase.org and have the class interview adults about this virtue.

- See the additional "Lesson Ideas for Teaching Virtue" at www.virtuebase.org.

- Perhaps hold a schoolwide assembly with a guest who has lived the virtue and can testify to its value (firefighters for fortitude, for example).

- Acknowledge and reward the virtue you observe.

## Class Meeting Three: Share Examples of Virtue

- Have students bring their stories/examples of adults who are role models of virtue and discuss the impact of these individuals on their lives in circle time.

- Assign students to write a story, fable, song, or poem about the virtue for the next class meeting. This can be a language-arts assignment. Collect the stories in advance of the meeting, and select one or two you think would be good to act out or share with younger audiences (or older ones). Then bring these to the students in the next meeting.

## Class Meetings Four-Six: Engage with the Student Projects

- Discuss the assignments you have selected and elicit student responses. Consider how these can be shared with other classes. Perhaps the school can have a monthly showcase of what students did to illustrate the virtue through language arts.

As your school selects virtues to work on for the year, staff coordinators should plan for schoolwide activities. These will be communicated to students as appropriate for each grade level. As mentioned previously in chapter 3, one teacher noted that after working on a virtue for several weeks, she was grading a student essay on an explorer in which the student wrote that the historical figure demonstrated the virtue of "seeing God in others" and explained why he thought this historical figure was virtuous. It is these kinds of small things that collectively express the importance of spirituality in everyday life. This is what it means to live a life of purpose, and this process brings deep happiness to those who work to elevate virtues in everyday living. As Father Benedict Groeschel states in *The Virtue Driven Life*:

> There is nothing wiser than to follow Christ. There is no surer way of happiness in this world than following the Gospel. The person who has sacrificed much in order to follow the su-

pernatural goals set by our Lord Jesus Christ may look unfortunate in the eyes of the world, but he or she will have greater interior peace. (Page 42)

It is easy to drown out the interior life by the daily pace we keep. Our children see us quickly getting up each morning, heading into the activities of the day, trying to keep up with information in our techno-saturated world — which is more than a full-time job! Then we rush home and through the evening activities before collapsing into bed, only to wake to the same pace the next morning. Adults at home could be helped by praying with their children and teaching virtue. They would be using the same themes the school uses in the year, and that three-legged stool that we mentioned in chapter 2 would be as strong as possible to "seat" God's word in our world.

# CHAPTER 12

# PUTTING IT ALL TOGETHER: RESTORING RELATIONSHIPS AND REPAIRING HARM

*"You will know them by their fruits.
Are grapes gathered from thorns, or figs from thistles?"*

Matthew 7:16

As you bring all the components together, it will be easy to see the progress you have made in shaping the climate of your school through virtue. These words will become the everyday language; and as you develop the vocabulary, students become responsive to their behavior first through the lens of their relationship with God, then with one another. It will become easier for them as they develop Christian critical thinking! They will be able to analyze their world in terms of virtue and faith, then recognize the goodness that they are called to and the happiness that God seeks for them.

In the second year of implementation, administer the survey again and compare and discuss the results to see where change must occur. Celebrating successes and rewarding progress will inspire more positive effort. Here are some stories that illustrate the full implementation and ways students have grown from the process.

## Gentleness

Two eighth-graders were climbing a tree after school while students were being picked up — and were in a high branch when a teacher spotted them. The ring of young onlookers was amazed at how high they had climbed, until the principal calmly called them down and dispersed the crowd. They came into the office, opened with a brief prayer to reflect on the harm they had caused, and discerned that the virtue to work on was gentleness — toward nature and toward younger students. Their discussion resulted in a full presentation on safety that was developed during their lunch period, the time they would have served the consequence according to school policy. The result: The younger students learned about safety and responsibility, and the boys were proud that they could help to enforce what they knew was ultimately a good and just policy regarding climbing trees near the parking lot. All the teachers reported a good outcome from the class meetings they held for the boys to make their presentation, and everyone learned from this experience.

## Unity

Two girls were arguing over the rules of a game. It eventually deteriorated into name-calling, with each one trying to "out-hurt" the other. This painful and unfortunate event was reported to the classroom teacher after recess. The two girls were called to the office, and the virtue they discerned after prayer was the need for kindness. Each had time to reflect on how badly the conversation went, how hurtful they were to each other, and what needed to happen next. They developed a plan to write a letter of apology to each other, which reflected deeper concerns about their relationship, with the intent to repair and restore their relationship with each other and the rest of the girls. The incident had polarized the girls in the class, and they needed to create unity through service. So, the girls decided to have a class meeting to discuss the damaging behavior and seek peace. The result gave more time to reflect on the ripple effect of cruelty in a classroom. While the girls struggled to get along with each other, they came up with strategies to help them be more aware when things were heating up and how to avoid confrontations.

## Prudence

A mother of a kindergartner contacted the school early on a Monday to report that over the weekend her young daughter had been watching cartoons, only to express in dismay, "Mommy, he's not using prudence!" When the mother questioned her about this unusual context, the girl proceeded to define prudence, describe the poor choice made by the character on television, and recommended a better behavior instead.

## Prayer

As the school was celebrating the retirement of two longtime staff members, the pastor asked that the children extend their hands and pray over them. When he asked, "What should we pray for?" the children immediately began to express intercession for virtues they had been taught in their class meetings.

## Forgiveness

A fifth-grade class had been struggling with mean-spirited behavior that was causing so much tension that instruction was compromised. Parents were reporting it to the principal, and teachers were concerned that the unhappiness of the students could have more serious repercussions. We called a meeting of parents and their fifth-grade children to discuss ways we treat one another, and all wished for a change for the better. So we agreed that the students would begin working on the virtue of forgiveness. In small groups, they would begin producing projects with that theme. Over a two-week period, the results were astounding. They performed skits, songs, and Scripture readings. One group created what appeared to be a science-fair project with a thesis statement regarding the cause and effect of kindness.

When parents came back for an evening titled "Showcase of Forgiveness," we all witnessed the students' profound understanding not only from the projects, but also from the Q & A panel they held at the end. They expressed the significance of the projects in changing their thoughts, words, and deeds toward one another — a tremendous improvement in the climate of their classroom.

## Appropriate Language

A young student was using inappropriate words in gym class. The teacher took him aside and asked if he thought there could be a better way to use words. The boy stated the need for kinder words, took time to reflect on the virtue of kindness, and proceeded to make posters for the gym that stood as reminders that redemption can follow mistakes.

## Perfect Timing

It was the evening of the Christmas program, and all the parents had come to see the play. Just before the performance, we presented a ten-minute message about virtue and gave parents a handout with simple tips to help integrate VBRD™ at home. Ideas such as this can be simple, offering easy suggestions for parents. Eventually, your students will be able to do this for themselves.

## The Restoration Process

When incidents occur, let common sense prevail. First, decide what "level" of severity the disruption is. As a staff member, or in your home with children, set some guidelines for what defines incidents as low-, mid- or high-level events. A low-level event might be a kindergartner saying something rude. A mid-level event might be an escalation of the rude comment when asked to stop. A high-level event may be pushing or shoving, or profanity and arguing. The process is as follows (see "The Restoration Process" in appendix 6 for additional details):

- Stop and pray to discern the virtue you are operating out of before speaking. This can be very spontaneous and brief, but it makes all the difference in what happens next!

- Approach the situation and stop the disruption with a neutral tone: "This is not acceptable," or "This needs to stop."

- Determine what just happened. If it is a small incident, this needs to be very informal and brief; if it is a larger one, decide whether it needs to be handled immediately and who else needs to be included.

- Be sure to protect the target of harm, assuring his or her needs are addressed. Do this, however, without drawing attention to the vulnerability that person may be feeling. Use neutral comments such as: "Here, let me help you pick up these books. Do you need a hand heading back to class?"

- Then you can deal with the one who was mistreating a peer by asking key questions. Pray together and note the virtue although this is not always practical or useful, so be sure to use discretion. This prayer should be simple: "Dear Jesus, help us through the virtues of _____ and _____ to work to bring peace and unity. Amen." (Peace and unity are two of my standard favorites when there is an argument or conflict.)

- Listen to all sides, empathizing and asking questions to clarify.

- Reflect on all possible solutions.

- Reach consensus about how to repair the harm, and then close with a prayer.

- Try the best option and check back later.

This simple formula can be used independently with older students. Have them write the summary of their meeting on the sheet, sign it, and go over it with their teacher. Students should always have an adult monitoring to ensure justice for the one harmed. This cannot be an option unless both parties agree to it, and adults must determine if there is an imbalance of power that may result in an unfair outcome. This is critical to assuring emotional safety and cannot be stressed enough!

## CONFERENCING CIRCLES

Getting parents involved is always recommended. Many times, parents are the first to hear of their child's experience, because children do not tell anyone at school. Why? Perhaps the biggest reason is that they are afraid they will be further harmed. Another reason is that adults at home may allow them to "blow off steam." This can present the child with the opportunity to tell the half-truth about what happened, omitting important details about the support provided by others or the role he or she played in escalating the conflict. Staff must intervene early and often to keep disruptions to a minimum. However, the school must also notify parents before the day ends when problems arise to reassure the parent that emotional safety is a priority. The school must also make sure the parent hears the entire story, including the steps the school has taken to establish and maintain justice.

When high-level incidents take place, or when a child is chronically involved in low-level incidents, a conference circle is recommended. This may require a meeting with one child and his or her parents. In other instances, after interviewing families individually, it may be advisable to bring them all together with a mediator trained in VBRD™ to provide the structure necessary for a successful outcome. All parties must adhere to the order provided in this model as outlined in "The Restoration Process" provided in appendix 6.

With proper training and experience in circle processes, you can aim to reach agreements between all parties desiring to improve conditions within their relationships. For instance, if two students have parents with conflicting values regarding expectations from their children, they may be receiving advice that causes further division and conflict in the classroom. Parents often suggest, "You just stay away from her!" But that can be difficult in a thirty-by-thirty-foot classroom. It can be confusing to a child who wants to get along with another student, or when the students involved in the conflict then compete for friendships, resulting in exclusion, hurtful gossip, or other mean-spirited behaviors. Well-intentioned parents must find empowerment in the effort to model virtue for their children. This can only bring about good for everyone! Prudence, using prayer and good judgment in choosing actions that support peace and unity in the classroom, would be an exemplary virtue to model in helping children appreciate and care for one another.

When teachers are cultivating virtue, they view their role with students as a holy ministry and vocation. Even on the days when patience runs thin, they are keenly aware of their close walk with God in sharing the responsibility for caring for students' emotional and physical needs. If parents and teachers are sharing this vision, all interactions become reverent, and the power struggles cease because both have the vision of virtue for themselves, the child, and others.

# CHAPTER 13

## MEASURING SUCCESS AND TELLING YOUR STORY

*"In this you rejoice, though now for a little while you may have to suffer various trials, so that the genuineness of your faith, more precious than gold which though perishable is tested by fire, may resound to praise and glory and honor at the revelation of Jesus Christ."*

1 Peter 1:6-7

THERE ARE TWO TRADITIONAL WAYS to show the success of your efforts.

### SURVEYS/EVALUATIONS

No matter how valiant your efforts in any setting, it is nearly impossible to determine success without a base of evidence. Teachers test students to see whether they have mastered a concept before teaching a new one. Those who provide funds want proof that their money is well spent. So, they require evidence of outcomes, typically in the form of a survey. Satisfaction surveys are a part of good customer-service practices.

When it comes to bullying prevention, many types of programs and practices exist, but rarely will these initiatives result in a 100 percent bully-free environment. Why? We are human — and therefore imperfect. Our propensity for sin causes us to fail in our relationships despite our best efforts. However, by documenting efforts, surveying students, parents, and staff, you will be able to identify what works and what needs work in the school community. Comparative survey results will bring your community to a greater understanding of ways their practices concerning harm have helped to create the best learning environment and fostered emotional safety both at home and at school.

Your discipline policy will be a dynamic, living document that adapts to the needs of your community. If adults are committed to ongoing circle processes and faith formation, ideas about ways to address harmful behaviors will continue to take shape. Most importantly, your outcomes should take adult behavior changes into consideration. If you are truly committed to this process, be sure to have one-on-one meetings with staff to discuss virtue formation and the fruit it can bear. Sometimes, personal circumstances can detract from good work performance and healthy interpersonal skills. It is times such as these that we can draw from the reserve we have developed in talking circles and prayer. These commitments to constructive behaviors must be guaranteed if your school is to succeed at creating a positive, safe, holy, school climate. Ongoing training in conflict skills for adults is a consideration when planning for your school.

The certification standards currently in place for VBRD™ include administering a baseline and annual surveys to comparatively measure the climate and practices both at home and at school. While some may worry that they will be scrutinized, judged, or held adversely accountable, this is not the intent of the model. Rather, we are looking for areas within each school environment that can be highlighted for success or for added effort in implementation with fidelity. Schools signing up to implement the model can review the survey instrument and work with the staff to determine how to begin collecting necessary data to show evidence of outcomes.

The surveys are administered electronically and sent to a neutral third party. Currently, Saint Louis University, under the leadership of Dr. John James, is collecting and tabulating the data. Establishing evidence of the effectiveness is critical for communities' investing time and resources in an effort such as this.

## CERTIFICATION

Schools are encouraged to receive appropriate training in order to meet requirements for certification. The steps are as follows:

- Contact the VBRD™ trainer for information through the Web site at virtuebase.org.

- Meet with appropriate individuals in your school community to determine readiness.

- Contact the VBRD™ trainer for a training schedule.

- Form a school VBRD™ Team with parents, staff, and administrator and set a date for training.

- Administer the survey.

- Begin formation for staff and parents.

- Begin virtue campaign planning.

- Begin working/meeting with students.

- Set all implementation steps into place and continue ongoing training requirements.

- Survey/document/track your progress.

- Apply for provisional certification for the school at the end of the school year.

- Begin planning for year two.

- Complete the necessary steps as in year one.

- At the end of year two, receive full certification if criteria are met.

- In year three, complete surveys and receive ongoing training.

- Complete all the documentation for required certification.

- Seek leaders within the school community to achieve trainer certification.

By maintaining certification efforts, schools will be positioned as leaders within their dioceses to support other schools in forming teams and training for certification. The network will offer all schools a clear vision for best practices in each aspect of implementation. The result will be an integration of faith and discipline that expresses a vibrant Catholic community of virtue.

This can be publicized and reported to school families so that there is no mistake about the importance of the work completed and offers a look at the work that lies ahead. Pockets of competency exist in almost every school environment, and finding success is important for continuing the effort. Many schools use VBRD™ as a marketing strategy to attract school families looking for a welcoming and safe learning environment.

Survey your community in the fall and follow up in the spring with an evaluation that reports progress in qualitative measures. Make contact early to have the survey link available. Everyone should be surveyed as quickly as possible to eliminate any possible disturbance to the base line data sampling.

## OTHER WAYS TO MEASURE OUTCOMES

You will learn best practices for tracking progress during training. Each school is given the tools for tracking individual interventions/restorations. Some schools develop their own online system, shared with others in their building, so that if a student is having trouble in one class, all other teachers who interact with the student can be aware of that fact and act accordingly.

Keep a "Book of Miracles," in which teams can record events when they meet. This can provide encouragement as good things that happen are recalled. These can be as simple as: Jason C. used a virtue in conversation with another student today in the proper context and as a compliment to another student. Mrs. C's class performed a play today on the virtue of hope for the third grade, and a student chose better behavior all week as she continued to talk about the positive impact of the play. Joey Z. asked a teacher to forgive him for the poor attitude he had been demonstrating.

These become the qualitative outcomes we are looking for. They can be added to the Student Tracking Forms that will show the change in behavior outcomes. So, refer to the "Virtue Recognition" form available at www.virtuebase.org and adapt as necessary for your school. These will need to be included in your documentation for certification if you are seeking the national recognition of your VBRD™ work.

When your school community has demonstrated the ability to integrate the complete program into school and home environments, you will see a dramatic change in the daily exchanges throughout parish life. Stay connected with your sporting, scouting, and other youth-serving organizations to assure fidelity to this model. The survey can be administered year after year, and hopefully the results will yield the desirable results. Remember that God does not take our successes and failures into account — but rather our faithfulness to the task. Living in virtue is a visible sign of your faith, and that of those you encourage.

For I am already on the point of being sacrificed; the time of my departure has come. I have fought the good fight, I have finished the race, I have kept the faith. Henceforth there is laid up for me the crown of righteousness, which the Lord, the righteous judge, will award to me on that Day, and not only to me but also to all who have loved his appearing. (*2 Timothy* 4:6-8)

# CHAPTER 14

## FINAL THOUGHTS

*"In all these things we are more than conquerors
through him who loved us."*

Romans 8:37

WHILE CERTIFICATION HAS THE ADVANTAGE of providing an ongoing support system and network for establishing and maintaining best practices, many readers may not have such an opportunity. What schools in the Saint Louis area have discovered is that the more they work with VBRD™, the more they want to learn. Many adults struggle with feeling confident in handling issues effectively, both at home and at school. Because each incident of harm has its own identifying marks, or "fingerprint," we can continually deepen our understanding of what it means to create an emotionally safe environment. Each circumstance requires a base of knowledge and skill unique to the individuals involved, and unique to the nature of the conflict.

Having been in this field for more than fifteen years, I find myself continually seeking deeper training, particularly in mediation and circle processes. Readers can do the same by staying current in their reading or attending training when possible. Many court systems initiate restorative justice programs, and individuals who work within those systems may offer circle trainings and conflict services. Services in mediation in local communities may also provide a source of training and support for restorative practices.

Cultivating virtue also needs to be a part of our everyday spiritual journey. It is not only for our own good, but also for the good of our neighbor. Think about how many times we have been affected by the words and actions of others — both in positive and negative ways. The world needs virtuous acts of kindness from parents, educators, parishioners, and community members. Our Christian call is to bring the real presence of Christ into the lives of those around us.

In my years of raising my young family, there was a point in which I experienced a holy longing, or the desire to know God in a deeper way. At the heart of my search was the desire to understand the true teachings of my faith, a longing for quiet reflection and prayer as I pursued these truths, and a deeper faith experience that could only be satisfied by yielding to the promptings of the Holy Spirit. The result has led me to this place in my journey with my work in VBRD™ that I share with you, the reader. It was my obedience to that still, small voice, and then actively surrendering my will and choosing to be swept up in a force bigger than myself. I was seeking the goodness of God.

As I listened to our Saint Louis shepherd, Archbishop Robert J. Carlson's *Keynote Address at the Religious Education Institute 2012,* he echoed my experience in a more formalized way. He identified three benchmarks for what he calls "an apologetics that can contribute to the New Evangelization today."

1.  **Orthodoxy** (True Church doctrine)

2.  **Contemplation** (Personal encounter with Christ)

3.  **Receptivity to the Holy Spirit** ("In the gifts and fruits, the Spirit is showing us the way that leads to life.")

VBRD™ can only be as effective as the most resistant staff person or parent will allow it to be. Many times we cannot fully invest ourselves in such an undertaking. Perhaps there is mental illness such as depression or a more serious affliction; or perhaps someone is stuck in unforgiveness and cannot see past blame. Maybe the brokenness within one's life simply is too consuming to see the way clear to grow at this point in time. Sometimes, adults struggle to feel adequate, or worthy of goodness because of their background or upbringing. In such cases, it is seemingly impossible to break through the barriers to find the goodness, or step outside ourselves to be loving and forgiving. You will know you have mastered the golden rule when you can push through with kindness in the face of unkindness. Mastering virtue, when we recognize that it is God who fuels us with grace, can motivate us in such times. Having a surge of grace when we have chosen to act in virtue is a reminder of God's goodness, fortifying us for the journey ahead.

Anyone can willingly choose to begin this process of self-improvement, and we can continually invite others to join us by simply doing three things:

1. **Cultivate virtue:** Become a student of virtue. Pray to have a holy hunger for a life of goodness for yourself and those around you. Seek out others willing to embark on this journey with you. You will not be disappointed.

2. **Commit to being constructive**: Through prayerful reflection linked with virtue, we are led to a deeper commitment to seeing the face of Christ in one another. We learn to discipline our thoughts, words, and deeds to bring hope and courage.

3. **Tell your story:** This is virtue activated by the Holy Spirit, animating us for the deeper call to evangelize others. This is what stirs the faith in others, leading them to imitate us because they are drawn to our joy. Then they show up more often at church, and choose to support the school or parish efforts.

Over time you will discover you are uncomfortable with negative, critical, or judgmental conversations. Gossip will cause you to feel uneasy. When you correct a child, you will find yourself practicing the virtue of gentleness. Accountability is still an expectation in behavior, but the learning experience is in fixing the mistake that was made rather than in the punishment you could assign.

These are signs that you are changing, and that is precisely where the world begins to change — within you. This book provides the template for this process, and the learning will last a lifetime. For schools choosing to enter the certification process by forming a team and seeking formal training, there are resources available and contact information provided in this book.

Each day will bring fresh adventures, and as you practice virtue, commit to constructive thoughts, words, and deeds, and then tell your story, you will be able to look behind you and see the seeds of good you have sown. People will want what you have, and that is what fills our classrooms and churches — agape love. It is the transforming power of God's love among us — that unmistakable joy that enables us to operate at a higher frequency. It is my hope that readers will be continually striving to experience this, and will grow a community around them to share the message. VBRD™ can be a practical set of skills implemented with fidelity in day-to-day circumstances that helps everyone to become their best for God, themselves, and for one another.

*"The one and only Gospel waits to be proclaimed by everyone together, in love and reciprocal esteem."*

(Pope Emeritus Benedict XVI, Vatican City, October 2, 2007)

# VIRTUE-BASED

# RESTORATIVE DISCIPLINE MODEL

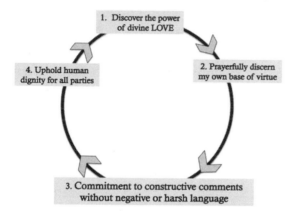

1. Discover the power of divine LOVE

2. Prayerfully discern my own base of virtue

3. Commitment to constructive comments without negative or harsh language

4. Uphold human dignity for all parties

1. Discover the power of divine LOVE

2. Prayerfully discern my own base of virtue

Mutual agreements support
Forgiveness and Reconciliation
through
Formation and Service

Injustices are recognized

Equity is restored

Make a better future

3. Commitment to constructive comments without negative or harsh language

4. Uphold human dignity for all parties

The circle illustrates the response to the needs of the whole person. Begin with the outer circle (at the left), then recognize the core of change within (below).

- Discover the power of divine love.
- Prayerfully discern my own base of virtue.
- Commit to constructive comments without negative or harsh language.
- Uphold human dignity for all parties.

ADAPTED FROM *DISCIPLINE THAT RESTORES*, BY RON AND ROXANNE CLAASEN

This work must first establish a clear understanding of the power of divine love.

Next, we must discern our own base of virtue.

The commitment to constructive language in all interactions must be modeled by adults and reinforced with students.

This then establishes the honor bestowed on everyone: upholding human dignity for all.

Then we can move toward the goal of reestablishing justice.

We must begin with the belief that forgiveness and reconciliation are the goal, and that these are accomplished through formation and service. Formation is the shaping of the will to conform to our Catholic faith. We use the outcomes of the restorative process to integrate service. For instance, we can hold students accountable for inappropriate language by having them post signs in the building about using kind words. Or, we can have students use their mistakes to teach younger students about a virtue that could help them avoid the problem in the future.

Once we see the inner circle (depicted in the bottom illustration on page 151) as our goal, then we help students do three things:

1. Identify the injustice. What went wrong?

2. Restore equity — making sure they have made things right. (Fair does NOT mean equal — you can talk about this.)

3. What can they guarantee about the future? Sometimes this is a written agreement.

POST THESE GUIDING PRINCIPLES throughout your school building as a visible sign of the commitment in your community. This list also can be adapted for your handbook for school discipline. Some schools ask students to recite the principles before going to recess, to pray, and, upon return from recess, to take a few minutes to note a virtue that they witnessed on the playground. These principles are:

1. **We will dedicate ourselves to living virtue.**

2. **We will support others in living virtue.**

3. **We will commit to constructive thoughts, words, and deeds.**

4. **When faced with challenges or conflict, we will find solutions that cultivate virtue for ourselves and for one another.**

In discussions with school staff, teachers, and students, talk about how to apply these principles:

1. **We will dedicate ourselves to living virtue.**
   a. We will learn about Catholic virtues from Scripture, the *Catechism of the Catholic Church*, and other resources.
   b. We will prayerfully discern one or two virtues that God may want us to cultivate. This will require prayer, journaling, and a deeper commitment to the sacramental life. You will know if this work bears fruit when others begin to see the change in you, and you notice a change in your relationships with others.

    c.   Dedicate time for more formation through reflection on Scripture and virtue. This can be done in small groups, in homes, or in other arranged settings.

2. **We will support others in living virtue.**
   a. We will share what we learn freely with others and encourage their journey in discerning virtue through the recommended resources.
   b. We will support one another and begin to pay genuine compliments when we see virtuous acts. We will encourage others by looking for the good in them.
   c. We will work together to support attendance at formation sessions and seek ongoing resources that encourage spiritual growth in our community.

3. **We will commit to constructive thoughts, words and deeds.**
   a. We will refrain from gossip, rumors, criticizing, and judgment, as these detract from the good name all people are given by God.
   b. When in community, we will build one another up, as we would want others to do for us in our absence.
   c. We will train our thoughts to be kind, and be prudent in our speech and temperate in our actions so as to achieve personal holiness within the community.
   d. We will choose to be kind about others, toward others, and with others.

4. **When faced with challenges or conflict, we will find solutions that further cultivate virtue for ourselves and for one another.**
   a. At all costs, we will uphold the human dignity assigned by God in dealing with one another.
   b. In our discussions, we can begin and end with prayer. We will see conflict as a virtue waiting to be cultivated, and when resolving conflict, we will declare the virtues in our discourse.
   c. As we resolve conflicts, we will commit to constructive thoughts, words, and actions, preserving the confidentiality and dignity of all parties.

# APPENDIX 3

## ADULT SESSIONS FOR
## VIRTUE FORMATION

### SESSION ONE

*Invitation to Virtue*

We are all connected within community, yet it is easy to feel disconnected and isolated. As Henri Nouwen explains in *Making All Things New: An Invitation to the Spiritual Life*, "our lives often seem like overpacked suitcases," bursting at the seams. We are all about the busyness of life, but sometimes we have to stop and ask ourselves the meaning of our efforts.

Purpose is a constant theme in creation — we are created for a purpose. To know our higher calling is to understand the purpose of our daily expense of energy. As we find our way toward our heavenly home, we seek God in everyday living in many ways.

For this first week of understanding virtue, we will read a small passage from Scripture three times. But first, we should begin with a prayer, asking God for an open heart and willing spirit.

### Scripture Reflection
"Put on then, as God's chosen ones, holy and beloved, compassion, kindness, lowliness, meekness, and patience." *Colossians 3:12*

The first time you read this passage, become familiar with the words. Ask God for guidance in understanding the message intended for you. Then read the same verse a second time, but more slowly. After a pause, read it again a third time, this time very slowly, pausing at each word, listening to the phrase, asking the Holy Spirit to illuminate your heart with inspiration. Then, reflect on the Scripture with these reflection questions:

How does this word or these words speak to me?: _____

_____

How can these words become guiding virtues in my role with others?

_____

How has God shown these virtues to me?_____

What can I do to return the favor that God has shown me? (Write a simple action plan for this week.) _____

_____

You may be asked to share your reflections on these virtues with others when gathering for discussion. What will you share?_____

_____

## SESSION TWO

*Invitation to Virtue*

EVERYTHING. God came to change everything. In the words of
Father Pedro Arrupe, S.J.:

> Nothing is more practical than finding God,
> That is, than falling in love in a quite absolute, final way.
> What you are in love with, what seizes your imagination will affect
>     everything.
> It will decide what will get you out of bed in the mornings,
> What you will do with your evenings,
> How you will spend your weekends,
> What you read,
> Who you know,
> What breaks your heart,
> And what amazes you with joy and gratitude.
> Fall in love, stay in love, and it will decide everything.
>                     (*Finding God in All Things: A Marquette Prayer Book*,
>                         Milwaukee: Marquette University Press, 2009)

When was the last time you asked God to truly enter your heart and
surrendered your own will and desires? As we reflect on how God has
created us for a design and purpose that is not our own, how much do
we allow God to determine our daily actions?

This week, reflect once again on the Scripture you read before, but read
it with a true sense of abandonment — not as if someone else is God's
chosen one, but that YOU are the chosen one. You were chosen by God
to clothe yourself in these virtues. But first, begin with a prayer, asking
God for an open heart and willing spirit.

### Scripture Reflection

"Put on then, as God's chosen ones, holy and beloved, compassion, kindness, lowliness, meekness, and patience." *Colossians* 3:12

Read this passage three times. The first time, simply become familiar with the words. The second time, read it more slowly. And the final time, read it even more slowly, resting on each word. Listen to the phrase, asking the Holy Spirit to help you surrender your own will and desire to hear God's voice.

How does this word or these words speak to me?: _____

_____

What virtue is God drawing to my attention, and why?_____

_____

Have I seen this virtue in others?_____

What can I do to return the favor that God has shown me? (Write a simple action plan for this week.) _____

_____

You may be asked to share your reflections on these virtues with others when gathering for discussion. What will you share? _____

_____

## SESSION THREE

*Invitation to Virtue*

Contemplating virtue is quiet pondering and watching with heightened awareness to see how virtue is activated around us. When we heighten our senses, we cannot help but increase our use of vocabulary about virtues in everyday life.

When we see others acting out of goodness, we are seeing virtue. When we speak about them and recognize the positive effect they have, we are recognizing the face of God in one another.

This week, reflect on how you have seen virtue around you — in thought, word, and deed. But first, begin with a prayer, asking God for an open heart and willing spirit.

### Scripture Reflection
"...forbearing one another and, if one has a complaint against another, forgiving each other; as the Lord has forgiven you, so you also must forgive." *Colossians* 3:13

Read this passage three times. The first time, simply become familiar with the words. The second time, read it more slowly. And the final time, read it even more slowly, resting on each word. Listen to the phrase, asking the Holy Spirit to help you surrender your own will and desire to hear God's voice.

How does this word or these words speak to me?: _____

_____

What does this passage tell me about my actions?_____

_____

Have I seen others truly practice the virtue of forgiveness?_____

_____

What can I do to return the favor that God has shown me? (Write a simple action plan for this week.)_____

_____

You may be asked to share your reflections on these virtues with others when gathering for discussion. What will you share?_____

_____

## SESSION FOUR

*Invitation to Virtue*

The words in the prayer below can express our desire to tirelessly seek God:

> Prayer is a whisper in my heart
> That ne'er gets expressed,
> This fire within me will not part
> And leaves me with no rest.
>
> Prayer is but a breath I take
> Then slowly do release;
> O God, it is but for your sake
> I silently await your grace.

When we pray, whether silently or aloud, God has already been patiently waiting for us. He tirelessly seeks us in every moment of our lives. He was there first, and it is our response to his presence that stirs the desire to pray.

In this session, reflect on the power of God's gift of forgiveness. No matter how many mistakes we make, no matter how many mistakes others around us make, God has already forgiven and paid the price through the gift of his son, Jesus. Begin with a prayer, asking God for an open heart and willing spirit.

### Scripture Reflection

"…forbearing one another and, if one has a complaint against another, forgiving each other; as the Lord has forgiven you, so you also must forgive." *Colossians 3:13*

Read this passage three times. The first time, simply become familiar with the words. The second time, read it more slowly. And the final time, read it even more slowly, resting on each word. Listen to the phrase, asking the Holy Spirit to help you surrender your own will and desire to hear God's voice.

How does this word or these words speak to me?: _____

_____

What does this passage tell me about my actions today? Who do I need to forgive?_____

_____

Have I seen others truly practice the virtue of forgiveness? Is there someone I need to thank for the gift of forgiveness? _____

_____

How can I live out the virtue of forgiveness as a return for the favor that God has shown me? (Write a simple action plan for this week.) _____

_____

You may be asked to share your reflections on these virtues with others when gathering for discussion. What will you share?_____

_____

## SESSION FIVE

*Invitation to Virtue*

Virtue in everyday life is evident, yet not spoken of. It is natural for us to say "thanks," or "I appreciate that," but less common for us to connect the actions of others or ourselves to virtue. When we decide to actively observe and recognize virtue, we are directing ourselves and others on the heavenly journey. So consider saying, "Thank you for that kind act," or "Thank you for your generosity — what a virtue!" In this way we are deliberately showing ways that virtue is lived out in everyday life.

In this session, reflect on the power of God's greatest virtue — love. This passage speaks about perfection. Life is far from perfect! Our difficulties and trials cause us agony and despair. But remember, perfection is in recognizing, giving, and receiving God's perfect virtue — love. Love never fails. Begin with a prayer, asking God for an open heart and willing spirit.

### Scripture Reflection

"And above all these put on love, which binds everything together in perfect harmony." *Colossians* 3:14

Read this passage three times. The first time, simply become familiar with the words. The second time, read it more slowly. And the final time, read it even more slowly, resting on each word. Listen to the phrase, asking the Holy Spirit to help you surrender your own will and desire to hear God's voice.

How does this word or these words speak to me?: _____

_____

What does this passage tell me about myself and those I love?_____

_____

Share about a time when you have truly experienced perfect love.

_____

_____

How can I live out the virtue of love as a return for the favor that God has shown me? (Write a simple action plan for this week.)

_____

_____

You may be asked to share your reflections on these virtues with others when gathering for discussion. What will you share?_____

_____

## SESSION SIX

*Invitation to Virtue*

If we think of the perfection of love as we know it in Scripture, how can we possibly experience that perfection on earth? How many times do our loved ones fail us? How many times do we fail them? Gossip, anger, resentment, or envy creeps into our minds and hearts, sometimes without our realizing it until it is too late. We have damaged a reputation or allowed our poor choice of words or actions to influence others to stand against someone.

As the *Catechism of the Catholic Church* describes in articles 2477, 2479 and 2507, respect for the reputation and honor of persons forbids all detraction and calumny in word or attitude. These sins offend against the virtues of justice and charity.

We can act against virtue (justice and charity) by choosing to gossip or create ill will against another. Calumny is a false statement against someone. So, if we ask ourselves whether we are practicing the virtue of love, we should consider how many comments we might choose to withhold out of love for self, others, and God.

This passage speaks about perfection. Begin with a prayer, asking God for an open heart and willing spirit.

### Scripture Reflection
"And above all these put on love, which binds everything together in perfect harmony." *Colossians* 3:14

Read this passage three times. The first time, simply become familiar with the words. The second time, read it more slowly. And the final time, read it even more slowly, resting on each word. Listen to the phrase, asking the Holy Spirit to help you surrender your own will and amplify your desire to hear God's voice.

How does this word or these words speak to me?_____

_____

Allow God to direct your thoughts about ways to show divine love.

_____

Share a time when you have truly experienced perfect love.

_____

How can I live out the virtue of love as a return for the favor that God has shown me?
(Write a simple action plan for this week.)_____

_____

You may be asked to share your reflections on these virtues with others when gathering for discussion. What will you share?_____

_____

# APPENDIX 4

## CIRCLE OF UNDERSTANDING
## ABOUT VIRTUE

This practice in adult circles should take fifteen minutes or less.

- Have your agreements in place before you begin.

- Open with a prayer.

- Ask each participant to check in with a single word.

Explain:

"For this circle of understanding about virtue, we will read this small passage from Scripture two times. Listen for the word or phrase that affects you and write about it briefly."

> Put on then, as God's chosen ones, holy and beloved, compassion, kindness, lowliness, meekness, and patience. (*Colossians* 3:12)

Each participant will write a response to the following:

- This is the word(s) that speaks to me and why: _____

_____

- These words can become guiding virtues in my role with others by: _____

  _____

- Go around the circle twice, passing the talking piece.
- Close with a prayer.

# APPENDIX 5

## LESSONS FOR TEACHING VIRTUE

1. Have students discuss what they know about virtue. Have the *Catechism of the Catholic Church*, "Part Three, Life in Christ" available. This section defines what a virtue is and identifies the main Catholic virtues, which are:

   - Faith
   - Hope
   - Charity (Love)
   - Temperance
   - Prudence
   - Fortitude
   - Justice

2. Create a mix-and-match game with the seven virtues listed above and their definitions. Make several sets so the class can work in small groups to see who can finish matching first. Then read the virtues and definitions out loud and discuss some specific behaviors associated with each. For instance, "What would be different about you if you practiced prudence?" "Would your classmates be able to tell?" "Why or why not?"

3. Have students find Scripture verses about each virtue (or assign specific virtues to groups). When they finish, have them share as

a class. Ask them to describe how we can be changed by living according to Scripture. Ask them if they know anyone who is modeling virtue, and how they see those virtues modeled. Have students interview people who model virtue, and ask them to share ways young people can grow in virtue — what advice can they give us?

4. Have students think about everyday situations in which they could intentionally practice virtue to change the way a situation is going, The situation could relate to dating, friendships, school, work, or family.

5. Have students spend one week praying about a virtue, then practicing five acts of that virtue daily and logging their actions. Then ask them to write a reflection on this experience.

6. Have students work in groups to create a sustainable project — a digital story, a PowerPoint presentation for other classes, or an activity that reflects the practice of virtue in your school.

   If your students create any kind of project showcase, I would love to see the result! (info@virtuebase.org)

## Steps to Restoration

1. Begin with prayer/confidentiality.

2. Identify the key virtues.

3. Determine what happened to bring us here today.

4. Ask what harm has been done and what can be done to repair it.

5. Ask how we will use this as an opportunity to grow in virtue.

6. Identify what we can expect in the future.

7. Review/write/sign any agreements.

8. Close with prayer and check back later.

## KEY QUESTIONS

- What happened? (What injustice occurred?)

- So what? (How will equity be restored?)

- Now what? (What are the future expectations?)

# APPENDIX 6

## THE RESTORATION PROCESS

Incidents will require different types of responses, depending on whether they are low-, mid- or high-level incidents. Remember: INTERVENE EARLY AND OFTEN! If you address the small disruptions, there will be fewer big ones!

### LOW LEVEL

Decide what constitutes a low-level incident: first-time events, disruptions that minimally affect others, talking out unintentionally, etc. Make a list and discuss it with students so all are clear about expectations. Also be clear about consequences, and be consistent.

Check your virtue: What is the guiding virtue that motivates you today?

- Make eye contact with the person(s) causing disruption.

- Stand next to the person(s) causing disruption.

- Use humor and lightheartedness whenever possible (though not at the expense of the student). ("Hey, did you know my virtue is patience today? I am really counting on you to help me.")

- Or say, "That needs to stop. Can we agree that it will?" When there is an expected standard of behavior, it is not necessary to say "please" or "thank you" regarding compliance.

- Or say, "Can we have a 'take back'?" Teach that a "take back" is a small matter, not necessarily requiring an apology or a more serious consequence. The goal is to intervene early and often to prevent escalating events.

- Or say, "I need an instant replay." This gives a student the opportunity to "rewind the clock" and erase a mistake such as throwing paper in class. When you get the replay, ask, "Why was that important to do?" Then note the virtue that was practiced in the replay. Virtue will focus on what we add to improve a circumstance. Rather than, "You're forgetting your virtues!" we might say, "I noticed forgiveness in that replay. Did you? How do you think that affected the people around you?"

## Mid Level

Mid-level incidents may include hurtful name-calling, or perhaps repeated events that would typically be low-level incidents. List what falls into this category and discuss consequences as you did before.

Check your virtue and pray silently when disruption occurs. When you have addressed the issue, BE SURE to contact parents to inform them of the incident (for both harmed and harmers — and witnesses if appropriate).

- Say, "I saw what happened, and it needs to stop. Am I clear?"

- Use humor: "Oh, hold on! I hear God calling! Yes — oh, we need (name virtue). Okay, God, I'll let them know. Thanks for calling. We love you, God! Bye! Okay everyone, we are supposed to be working on (virtue). Can we try again? What do we need to do?" (Get agreement before moving on.)

- Or say, "Let's take time here to ask for help. Would you like to lead the prayer or should I?" (Then say a brief prayer about help with a virtue.)

- Or say, "What is happening here? Is there harm or mistreatment to anyone?" (Give students time to think. This will be a work in progress as everyone learns this restorative model, so be patient as children — and adults — learn.)

- When necessary, arrange to speak with students individually or as a group. Have a circle meeting to establish three things:
  - An injustice occurred. What was it?
  - Restore equity: How can we make things as right as possible?
  - Guarantee a better future: What can we do to help each other? (Don't forget to ask what might be needed from YOU to help in the future.)

Be sure to write down and sign any agreements, and include parents if necessary. It also can be helpful to have parents meet separately with an adult at school to discuss ways to support the effort for peace and unity.

Having regular parent meetings at varying grade levels is an important step in prevention. These can give adults the solidarity necessary to help children with the formative process. At times, it is good to have parents of children who struggle with compliance come in for virtue-driven parenting tips and strategies. This will greatly improve your school environment.

## HIGH LEVEL

These behaviors require a more rigorous process. Your most important task is to help young people OWN the problem and the solution. The only way to do this is to learn "the art of the question." You will establish critical-thinking skills by asking the student to do the work. The better you get at asking good questions, the less talking and "lecturing" you will need to do. Over time, this will become easier and easier.

Circle conferences and restoration circles will be a necessary part of handling high-level incidents. If expulsion is an option, be sure to have a mental-health assessment in place prior to coming to the circle.

When multiple students are involved, it is important to interview each one individually with parents. Remember to establish the three keys to restoration:

1.  An injustice occurred. What was it?

2.  Restore equity: How can we make things as right as possible?

3.  Guarantee a better future: What can we do to help each other? (Don't forget to ask what might be needed from you to help in the future.)

Before bringing all the students and parents together, be clear about what each wants from the conference. If there is not willingness to apologize and make things right, do not bring the parties together. The only way to restore equity is to operate out of the virtues of humility and forgiveness.

What is the guiding virtue? Write it down where others can see it. This is a good reminder for you and those around you.

- Say, "This is unacceptable, and it needs to stop." Do you have time in that moment to deal with the problem? If so, call the student conference immediately. Otherwise, decide what procedural steps need to happen — sending students to the office, or having students removed from the environment to protect other students.

- Establish safety for the harmed. Make sure these individuals do not need physical care. Privately address the harmed individuals so they are not humiliated further. Find out what is necessary for them to reestablish a sense of safety. But be sure to address the harmer first.

It is important to emphasize that God gives us indestructible dignity. While others may attempt to hurt us, we must remember that the inviolable human dignity given to every human person cannot be destroyed. This is a powerful message that preserves our sense of dignity when others attack us. We cannot be damaged by the words or actions of those who mistreat their peers within our spiritual selves. Physical harm does not activate a loss of dignity. Rather, harm requires us to take steps to repair and restore, thus reestablishing equity, emotional and physical safety, and assuring a better future. Adults must do everything possible to promote human dignity and reverence for the human person.

Refer to *Format for Restoration Conference* (see appendix 7).

## FORMAT FOR RESTORATION
## CONFERENCE

**#1 Key to Successful Conferences: Allow them to be child-driven as much as possible.** The facilitator should be simply a "traffic director" to keep people on course and virtuous in their speech.

You will need to determine who should come to the table — individual families, or several involved families.

When there is a high-level incident, or lesser incidents that cumulatively contribute to the need for a high-level conference, here is the process:

1.  First establish the extent of harm and have individual conversations with those involved.
    *   Use the restorative processes already discussed/practiced.
    *   Be sure all parties want resolution and that appropriate apologies can be expressed before bringing everyone together. It is essential to emotional safety that those harmed will have harm repaired and equity reestablished through this process.
    *   Contact parents and ask for their support in restoring peace (be sure to state your virtue — both as a reminder to you and to the other person). Then establish a time to meet with each family separately, first, if necessary.

2.  Prepare for all parties to be seated around a table.
    - Have guidelines written and read/explain them before beginning.
    - Have paper and pencils/pens available.
    - Have five-by-seven-inch sheets of unlined paper and markers.
    - A talking piece or other religious symbol.
    - Have ready guiding Scripture (*Colossians* 3:12-15).

3.  Begin by explaining why you are gathered, stating the problem you wish to solve.

4.  Pray.

5.  Go over guidelines:
    - We will speak one at a time without interruption.
    - We may ask for clarification of what someone has said, or we may be asked to restate what we have heard to be sure there are no misunderstandings.
    - I will not discuss what is said here outside this room. Out of respect for the dignity of each person here, I would ask the same of you. However, I cannot control what you do. So, please consider the dignity of each person here as you leave.
    - Our comments today should be mindful of the dignity of each person. So, please be sure to use words that express virtue — or goodness.
    - Can we agree to these things?
    - Next, we must establish what virtues — or holy habits — we are working to demonstrate here for one another. In other words, what qualities do we want to show our children in the way we interact? (Share yours again: "I want to show my commitment to peace and unity here as we listen and speak."). Write the word or words on a five-by-seven-inch piece of paper with marker. Have everyone write and tell what they have written.

- Can we agree to uphold these virtues? If we need to be reminded of these during the conversation, I will call us back to them. Is that agreeable to you?

6. State these four truths:
   1. There may be more than one perspective, so we need to be open to the perspective of others.
   2. This will not be over after this discussion today. So, we need to continue to ask God to open our hearts to new ways of thinking and seeing.
   3. Stay present to the process. We will all have to change something we are doing in order to improve the way we are treating each other.
   4. We will need to stay focused on doing better — each of us individually, and all of us collectively. That will mean we keep talking to each other with the intent to make things better, even when it might not FEEL better at the time. The ongoing conversations can help our children. We can agree to disagree without being disagreeable.

7. The conversation should focus on three areas that can be illustrated for all to see:
   1. What injustice occurred — who was harmed by it.
   2. What will be done to restore equity — how can we make it right?
   3. How can we guarantee a better future? This will involve a written contract with signatures as appropriate.

   - Ask for a volunteer to begin, and have others be sure to actively listen by repeating what they hear.
   - Be sure to direct parties to avoid "You" statements that are accusatory, and stick to facts rather than perceptions.
   - Allow equal time for listening and speaking.
   - If necessary, take breaks if tempers are beginning to flare.

- Continue to focus on solutions and the shared goals rather than the details of hurtful events.
- Once all three areas are discussed fully, craft an agreement that is signed by all.
- It may be necessary to meet with adults separately to be sure they will support the commitment of the children, acknowledging that peace and unity are critical to harmony at school and at home.

8.  Bringing closure.
    - When agreements are reached, check in with everyone.
    - Write down/sign any necessary documents.
    - By allowing students to do most of the talking, they are learning needed skills.

**Some good points that seem to be helpful in working with adults:**

1.  Because perceptions and intentions may not match, don't assume to understand what motivates another's actions.

2.  For every negative comment about someone, ask for three positive statements to offset the detraction from another's good name.

3.  Learn to surrender the need to "win" for the goal of teaching young people to live in harmony, a good thing that has intrinsic rewards.

4.  Explain that a good, sincere apology can go a long way even if it is for something done as a reaction to an injustice to oneself. For instance, if I am called a name, and I hit someone back, I am responsible for hitting, even though I was harmed by the humiliation of name-calling. We are responsible for the way we respond to the world around us.

5.  Closure should involve an intentional positive expectation in the future. Perhaps encourage a time and place to meet again, or an "assignment" of unspoken kind acts of service.

# APPENDIX 8

## VIRTUE CAN AID US
## WITH VIOLENCE

WHEN UNEXPLAINABLE ACTS OF VIOLENCE PLAGUE US, God provides many opportunities to bring comfort and healing. The theological virtues of faith, hope, and love can teach all of us, both adults and children, about resiliency, which is critical to recovering from the affects of trauma. The intentional practice of virtue can be transforming and life-giving to those open to seeking God in difficult circumstances.

The three theological virtues are supernatural because they are 1) revealed by God and known by faith, 2) infused into our souls by God (see *CCC* 1813), and 3) intended to bring about our participation in the divine nature. They are called "theological" because they have God as their object. "Faith, hope, and love" mean faith in God, hope in God, and love of God and of neighbor for God's sake. Here are some simple ways to respond within the framework of virtue to the difficult questions we ask when unexplainable events occur.

1.  ***Why did it happen?*** So many things in life are unexplainable. Many times, we simply don't have enough information, or we don't always have accurate information to fully understand the "why." We attempt to draw clarity from the circumstances so we can make sense out of senseless acts. We want to learn ways to prevent future harm from happening to others. However, our ability to predict and prevent violence has its limits. That is where the virtue of faith resides. While we know that there are sad things we will

all experience, faith teaches us that when we can't understand loss, death, or suffering, and that God is with us to help us get through difficult times.

**Faith:** The gift of faith is knowing that there is an infinitely good God. Even in the worst experiences, it provides comfort in hardship in natural and supernatural ways. We are given the gift of faith from the moment of conception to share in the divine nature of God (see also *CCC* 1814).

> *Lord, to whom shall we go? You have the words of eternal life.* (John 6:68)

*Natural* comforts are found in the kind and compassionate acts of those who take care of us by holding our hand, hugging, or feeding us, and making sure our physical and emotional needs are met. The *supernatural* acts of God are discovered through the Holy Spirit, the great Comforter. Faith allows us to experience the peace that passes all human understanding. This is an unexplainable peace each of us can experience in unique ways. It is unquestionably the hand of God activating the virtue of faith.

> *Do not let your hearts be troubled. You have faith in God; have faith also in me.* (John 14:1)

Prayer is the best way to make sense out of experiences that seem senseless. Prayer allows us to see the natural goodness around us, and to experience the supernatural wonders of God's presence in the world today.

2.  ***How can we avoid a similar situation?*** Learning from tragedy can prevent further tragedy, but we cannot always predict or prevent suffering. While we have many safeguards in place in our schools and procedures to follow, there will always be a degree of uncer-

tainty about what may happen. We must be vigilant. But, we must also trust in God to provide us with what we need each day.

**Hope:** Believing in things unseen, and the possibility that the future holds good things for us. By fostering the virtue of *hope*, we can help one another avoid despair, which is the loss of all hope.

> *In my Father's house there are many dwelling places. If there were not, would I have told you that I am going to prepare a place for you?*
> *And if I go and prepare a place for you, I will come back again and take you to myself, so that where I am you also may be.*
> (John 14:2-3)

Hope is activated in the *natural* world by the things we look forward to such as birthdays, Christmas, or fun activities we plan. In the *supernatural* world, hope resides in knowing there is a place God has prepared for us. Through Jesus, that eternal home is at the end of our journey here on earth. Our faith teaches us that those who are taken from us, whether suddenly or after a long life, can find comfort in knowing they will no longer suffer what we endure in our earthly life. Our prayers can help others who are in despair, and can also help those who have left this life to gain eternal life.

**Love (or charity):**

1. ***What should we tell our children?*** Tell them about the theological virtue of love (see also *CCC* 1822). We don't always understand why things happen. We do everything we can to prevent tragedies from happening to them, and we love them very much. But, God loves them even more. When things seem to be going wrong, pray to the Blessed Mother for comfort, and call on the name of her son Jesus, our companion and brother.

> *Perfect love casts out fear.* (1 John 4:18)

When we cannot be there for our children, or things cannot be perfect, we must trust our perfect mother, Mary, to protect each of us. We should also call on St. Joseph, to bring the supernatural love that provides comfort and peace. Prayer is what we offer as our best response in all circumstances. The Hail Mary, the Our Father, and the Prayer of St. Francis are all appropriate in practicing the theological virtues. Give your children an extra hug and kiss, and tell them how much you love them. Love is the greatest gift and the greatest weapon we have.

*So faith, hope, love remain, these three; but the greatest of these is love.* (1 Corinthians 13:13)

# About the Author

LYNNE LANG is director of school climate for Catholic schools in the Archdiocese of Saint Louis.

# Resources

Bluestein, Jane. *Creating Emotionally Safe Schools*, Health Communications, Inc., 2001

Fein, Vossekuil, Pollack, Borum, Modzeleski, Reddy. *Threat Assessment in Schools Guide.* Washington, D.C., 2001.

Goleman, Daniel. *Emotional Intelligence.* New York: Bantam Books, 1994.

Kreeft, Peter. *Making Choices: Practical Wisdom for Everyday Moral Decisions.* Cincinnati: Servant Books, 1990.

Kreeft, Peter. *Virtues and Vices.* New Haven, CT: Catholic Information Service, Knights of Columbus Supreme Council, 2001.

Latimer, Jeff, Dowden, Craig, and Muise, Danielle. "The Effectiveness of Restorative Justice Practices: A Meta-Analysis," *The Prison Journal*, 85:2, June 2005: 127-144.

McCold, P., and Wachtel, T. "In Pursuit of Paradigm: A Theory of Restorative Justice. Paper presented at the XIII World Congress of Criminology, Rio de Janeiro, Brazil, August, 2003.

Minow, Martha. *Between Vengeance and Forgiveness: Facing History after Genocide and Mass Violence.* Boston: Beacon Press, 1998.

Nathanson, D. "Affect Theory and the Compass of Shame." In *The Widening Scope of Shame.*, edited by M. Lansky and A. Morrison, Hillsdale, NJ: The Analytic Press, Inc.

Nouwen, Henri. *Making All Things New: An Invitation to the Spiritual Life*, New York: HarperCollins, 1981.

Paul VI, Pope. *Humanae Vitae,* encyclical letter on the regulation of birth. Rome: Vatican Information Services, 1968.

Peterson, C. & Seligman, M. *Character Strengths and Virtues: A Handbook and Classification.* New York: Oxford University Press, 2004.

Storey, Peter. "A Different Kind of Justice: Truth and Reconciliation in South Africa," *The Christian Century*, September 10-17, 1997.

Sullivan, Dennis, and Tifft, Larry. *The Handbook of Restorative Justice: A Global Perspective.* Oxford, England: Taylor and Francis Books, 2006.

Tomkins, S.. "Shame," in *The Many Faces of Shame,* edited by D.L. Nathanson. New York: Norton, 1987.

Wachtel, T. "The Next Step: Developing Restorative Communities." Paper presented at the Seventh International Conference on Conferencing, Circles, and other Restorative Practices, Manchester, England, November, 2005.

International Institute of Restorative Practices, http://www.iirp.edu/what-is-restorative-practices.php.

"Tree of Virtues" and "Tree of Vices," *Beinecke MS 146*. Beinecke Rare Book and Manuscript Library at Yale University. http://brbl-archive.library.yale.edu/exhibitions/speculum/3v-4r-virtues-and-vices.html